CAMPAIGN • 249

VERCORS 1944

Resistance in the French Alps

PETER LIEB

ILLUSTRATED BY PETER DENNIS

Series editor Marcus Cowper

First published in Great Britain in 2012 by Osprey Publishing,
Midland House, West Way, Botley, Oxford OX2 0PH, UK
44-02 23rd St, Suite 219, Long Island City, NY 11101, USA

E-mail: info@ospreypublishing.com

© 2012 Osprey Publishing Ltd

OSPREY PUBLISHING IS PART OF THE OSPREY GROUP.

A CIP catalogue record for this book is available from the British Library.

ISBN: 978 1 84908 698 1
E-book ISBN: 978 1 84908 699 8
ePub ISBN: 978 1 78096 116 3

Editorial by Ilios Publishing Ltd, Oxford, UK (www.iliospublishing.com)
Page layout by: The Black Spot
Index by Fionbar Lyons
Typeset in Myriad Pro and Sabon
Maps by Bounford.com
3D bird's-eye view by The Black Spot
Battlescene illustrations by Peter Dennis
Originated by PDQ Media, Bungay, UK
Printed in China through Worldprint Ltd.

12 13 14 15 16 10 9 8 7 6 5 4 3 2 1

DEDICATION

To my dear wife Tina.

ARTIST'S NOTE

Readers may care to note that the original paintings from which the color
plates in this book were prepared are available for private sale. The
Publishers retain all reproduction copyright whatsoever. All enquiries
should be addressed to:

Peter Dennis, Fieldhead, The Park, Mansfield, Notts, NG88 2AT, UK

magieh@ntlworld.com

The Publishers regret that they can enter into no correspondence upon this
matter.

THE WOODLAND TRUST

Osprey Publishing are supporting the Woodland Trust, the UK's leading
woodland conservation charity, by funding the dedication of trees.

ACKNOWLEDGEMENTS

This book could not have been written without the substantial help of many
people. I would like to thank my French colleagues who shared their
knowledge with me or granted me free access to their photo archives. These
were Pierre-Louis Fillet (Curator of the Musée de la Résistance in Vassieux),
Général de division (retired) Guy Giraud (Union des Troupes de Montagne),
Gilles Vergnon (Université Lyon II), Alain Raffain, Philippe Huet and Ayamar
de Galbert. Many Germans have also given me support as well as photos
from 1944, especially Franz Penzkofer (Archives of the Kameradenkreis der
Gebirgstruppe), Heinrich Henning, Karl Moser (both of the veterans'
association 8. Gebirgs Division) and Hans Hammer. Stijn David has kindly
given me permission to use some of his private German glider photos.
I was also fortunate to exchange many ideas about the Vercors with Paddy
Ashdown. My colleagues at RMA Sandhurst, Chris Mann, Matthias Strohn
and Stephen Walsh have all given advice on the manuscript with regards to
content and style; they prevented me from the worst abuses of the English
language. At Osprey Publishing Marcus Cowper followed the production of
the book with patience, help and advice. I am very grateful that he strongly
encouraged and supported my case and accepted a rather unusual topic on
irregular war into the Osprey Campaign Series.

IMPERIAL WAR MUSEUM COLLECTIONS

Many of the photos in this book come from the Imperial War Museum's
huge collections which cover all aspects of conflict involving Britain and
the Commonwealth since the start of the twentieth century.

These rich resources are available online to search, browse and buy at
www.iwmcollections.org.uk. In addition to Collections Online, you can
visit the Visitors Rooms where you can explore over 8 million photgraphs,
thousands of hours of moving images, the largest sound archive of its
kind in the world, thousands of diaries and letters written by people
in wartime, and a huge reference library. To make an appointment call
(020) 7416 5320, or email mail@iwm.org.uk. Imperial War Museum
www.iwm.org.uk

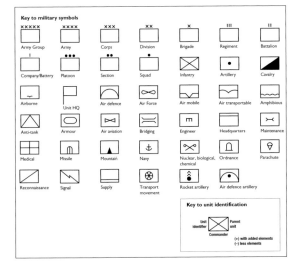

CONTENTS

NOTES ON TERMINOLOGY FFI–MAQUIS

The terms 'FFI' and 'Maquis' often give rise to confusion amongst readers of books on the French Resistance. Whilst the FFI were formed in early 1944 to give the Resistance a military character, the Maquis stemmed from escapees of the STO who were initially unarmed and more or less outlaws. The word, however, soon became synonymous with the armed resistance against the occupation and Vichy. Generally, Resistance fighters with a military background favoured the term 'FFI', whilst those with a civilian origin preferred 'Maquis'. For the sake of simplicity both terms are used synonymously in this book. The communists often preferred to call themselves 'partisans', while the Germans called the FFI/Maquis/partisans either 'terrorists' or 'bandits'.

NOTES ON PHOTOS

Finding photos for this book turned out to be a real challenge in many ways. Soldiers from both sides, German and French, were actually forbidden to take photos for security reasons. As a consequence, the number of photos from the actual fighting in the Vercors and the Tarentaise is very limited. However, a number of men ignored the ban and smuggled their snapshots back home.

ABBREVIATIONS

AS	Armée Secrète (Secret Army)
BA	Bundesarchiv
BCA	Bataillon de Chasseurs Alpins (Mountain Infantry Battalion)
BCRA	Bureau Central des Renseignements et d'Action (Central Office for Intelligence and Action)
FFI	Forces Françaises d'Intérieur (French Forces of the Interior)
FTPF	Francs-Tireurs et Partisans Français (French Free-Shooters and Partisans)
GMR	Groupes Mobiles de Réserve
HSSPF	Höherer SS-und Polizeiführer (Higher SS and Police Commander)
IWM	Imperial War Museum
KdS	Kommandeur der Sicherheitspolizei und des Sicherheitsdienstes (Commander of the Security Police and the Security Service)
KG	Kampfgeschwader (Combat Wing)
LLG	Luftlandegeschwader (Airborne Wing)
MRV	Musée de la Résistance in Vassieux
MTM	Musée des Troupes de Montagne
OG	(US) Operational Group
ORA	Organisation de Résistance de l'Armée (Resistance Organization of the Army)
OSS	Office of Strategic Services
RAF	Royal Air Force
Sipo/SD	Sicherheitspolizei und Sicherheitsdienst (Security Police and Security Service)
SOE	Special Operations Executive
SPOC	Special Projects Operations Centre
STO	Service du Travail Obligatoire (Forced Labour Service)
USAAF	United States Army Air Force
USMC	United States Marine Corps

ORIGINS OF THE CAMPAIGN

It appeared to be one of the biggest mysteries of military history; in little more than six weeks during late spring 1940 the German Wehrmacht overran the French Army – an army that had previously been regarded as the best in the world. The new French government under the old Maréchal Philippe Pétain had to agree to an armistice with its arch-enemy on 22 June 1940, in exactly the same railway carriage in which the 1918 armistice had been signed. France was largely occupied; the north and the west of the country came under German military administration, whereas the south remained officially independent under Pétain's authoritarian regime and was often named after its capital: Vichy France. She was allowed to keep an army of 100,000 men and, even in the German-occupied north, her administration and her police.

Despite the shocking defeat, many Frenchmen rallied around the old Maréchal, the hero of the battle of Verdun in 1916. After all, he had saved

Hitler and Pétain. The symbol of the Vichy French collaboration with Nazi Germany: the Vichy head of state Maréchal Philippe Pétain (left) and Adolf Hitler meet in Montoire, October 1940, to discuss France's role in the 'New Europe'. (BA, 183 H-25217)

France with his steadiness in those dark days of World War I. In contrast the socialist-communist government of the 'Popular Front' was widely regarded as having betrayed the country by neglecting the armament of the army in the face of the German threat in the 1930s, and the communists had sabotaged the nation's war efforts in 1939–40 against the Soviet-allied German enemy. These thoughts shot through the minds of many Frenchmen in the early days of the German occupation and Pétain's authoritarian regime, with his Révolution Nationale and the slogan 'travail, famille, patrie' (work, family, homeland), promised to sort out the perceived mess. Certainly, most of the French still despised or hated the Germans, even though, during the occupation, their soldiers behaved surprisingly correctly. However, in the early days of the occupation many French considered the Boche a lesser evil than those they perceived as enemies within French society, namely the communists and foreign Jews.

Almost no other aspect of the German occupation in France is as controversial and as heatedly discussed as the French–German collaboration. It is certainly not helpful to view it in stark black and white terms. Between 1940 and 1942 it seemed fairly unlikely France would soon be liberated and hence most ordinary Frenchmen adopted a wait-and-see attitude, which was later called *attentisme*. The presence of the occupiers could not just be ignored and, on a daily basis, the French had to cooperate with them to a certain degree or at least accommodate them. The Vichy government collaborated for a different reason; in the first months and years in particular it tried to comply with the Germans in many ways in order to reserve a privileged place for France in Hitler's Europe. This does not mean that Vichy politicians were pro-German, often quite the opposite. However, a similar attitude towards common enemies, such as communists or foreign Jews (in contrast to French Jews), helped to forge this German–French collaboration. In security matters, for example, French police forces maintained law and order, which allowed the Germans to run the country with a minimum of their own forces for a maximum outcome. Furthermore, Vichy maintained its responsibility for the entire civil administration system; the Germans only intervened if they felt their interests threatened. Although the Vichy collaboration, and particularly the collaboration of its police forces, dwindled away after 1942–43, the French administration kept on working for the Germans until summer 1944.

In autumn 1942 the Allied landings in French North Africa reversed the entire strategic situation in the Mediterranean. Vichy France's army had offered little resistance to the Allied invasion and Hitler feared the southern French coast could provide the Allies with a springboard into western Europe. Thus German (and Italian) troops entered into the hitherto unoccupied zone on 11 November 1942. The French Army was dissolved, but the Germans decided to keep the police force and the administration alive. Officially Vichy even remained the legal government in France, but in reality it held little power, becoming a mere puppet for the occupiers. Two other events changed the domestic situation in France over the course of 1943. Firstly, it became more and more obvious Germany would not win the war, having suffered one setback after the other: the capitulation of 6. Armee in Stalingrad in February and of Heeresgruppe Afrika in Tunis in May, the failed summer offensive at Kursk in July, the Allied landings on Sicily and southern Italy in July and August, Italy's capitulation in September and finally the Wehrmacht's constant withdrawals on the eastern front. Secondly, Vichy's strategy of

accommodation and collaboration had led to a dead end and had not brought any tangible success. The situation worsened when Vichy passed a law introducing a compulsory labour service, the Service du Travail Obligatoire (STO), on 16 February 1943. Young Frenchmen had to go to Germany to work in factories and the armament industry. The STO was the last nail in the coffin; Vichy had lost its credibility in the eyes of the French public, even though Maréchal Pétain still enjoyed widespread popularity. Many young people decided to dodge the STO and sought refuge in remote rural areas, particularly in southern France. The Maquis was born! Although initially the Maquisards were neither automatically Resistance fighters nor organized in any form, the Resistance was able to recruit from a large reservoir of manpower. The term Maquis would soon become a synonym for the armed Resistance in general.

The beginnings of the Resistance were difficult and rocky. Of course, there was a French general named Charles de Gaulle, residing in London, who had appealed to his countrymen on BBC radio on 18 June 1940. He reminded them that France had lost a battle, but not the war, and that it still had powerful allies, an empire and a navy. However, de Gaulle's emotional and visionary words in his *Appel du 18 Juin* remained largely unheard in his home country. The communists joined the Resistance only after the German invasion of the Soviet Union on 22 June 1941 and launched a series of assassination attempts on individual German soldiers. As a consequence German military commanders shot a small number of hostages but, after Hitler's personal intervention, the number of victims rose to the hundreds. In the end, the assassination attempts were futile; the communists were forced to realize that the French public was not yet wholly in support of acts of resistance.

Two German officers and two NCOs take a stroll in the town of Neufchâteau, Eastern France, August 1940. The first three years of the German occupation were marked by a surprising degree of calm and very little action from the French Resistance. (Author's collection)

A lightly wounded officer briefs a group of Maquisards, probably in the Vercors. The uniforms are from the Chantiers de Jeunesse, a compulsory Vichy French paramilitary youth organization, with no armament. The armistice of 1940 forbade conscription, but the Vichy government deemed the newly created Chantiers a suitable substitute for military training. Significantly, the instructors were usually former regular or reserve officers. However, some Chantiers groups turned against the regime and became the core of future Maquis groups. (Alain Raffain)

The Germans, too, held back the growth of the French Resistance movement. The Sicherheitspolizei und Sicherheitsdienst (Sipo/SD, Security Police and Security Service or, more commonly, the Gestapo) were able to penetrate Resistance cells and remove key personalities owing to an effective network of French agents and 'turned' Resistance fighters. In addition, torture was commonplace and widely used in interrogation. The most significant loss for the Resistance was certainly Jean Moulin, who had united various Resistance movements. He was captured and finally executed on 8 July 1943. Another big setback was the arrest in summer 1943 of Général Charles Delestraint, the leader of the Gaullist armed wing, the Armée Secrète (AS, Secret Army); deported to Germany he died in Dachau concentration camp just a few days before the liberation on 19 April 1945.

The history of the French Resistance would not be complete without mentioning the support of the Western Allies. On 22 July 1940 Winston Churchill created the Special Operations Executive (SOE) to 'set Europe ablaze'. This meant instigating rebellion in German-occupied countries as well as collecting intelligence from these areas. The US followed suit on 13 June 1942 with the foundation of the Office of Strategic Services (OSS), the forerunner of today's CIA. Both Western Allies maintained a special interest in the French Resistance movement as they knew France would one day be the focus of their landings and therefore the key theatre of war in the west. SOE and OSS also attempted to channel the political factions of the underground movements, because the Allies certainly did not welcome communist dominance of the French Resistance. However, de Gaulle, as the leader of the Free French, always viewed the work of the SOE and OSS in France with a critical eye, because he considered their actions illegitimate on French soil. The SOE and OSS sections dealing with occupied France were located either in London or, after 1943, in Algiers ('Massingham' for the SOE). Of course, the Free French in London could not just sit on the sidelines and they set up their own intelligence branch, the Bureau Central de Renseignements et d'Action (BCRA, Central Office for Intelligence and Action), which in the end turned out to be perhaps the most efficient of the three rival Allied intelligence services. Allegedly 80 per cent of the intelligence used for D-Day came through the channels of the BCRA.

For a long time the Resistance movement was still split with regard to strategy. Three major movements eventually prevailed: the communists with their fighting arm, the Francs-Tireurs et Partisans Français (FTPF, French Free Shooters and Partisans), endorsed and pushed for further immediate action to give themselves a higher public profile (moreover, these actions were intended to trigger harsh German reprisals and cause a spiral of violence); in contrast, the Gaullists, as the second most important Resistance group, favoured organizing, training and arming their Armée Secrète for the time being, wanting to embed their plans into the overall

Allied strategy and strike only in concert with the expected Allied landings; finally, the third Resistance group was the Organisation de Résistance de l'Armée (ORA, Resistance Organization of the Army) made up of former military personnel – politically mostly conservative, they sought to turn the Resistance groups as soon as possible into a regular army. Ideologically the ORA represented the exact opposite of the communists: this emnity hampered the creation of a single French Resistance movement for a long time and the antagonism would continue even after the liberation of France. Eventually the FTPF, the AS, ORA and other smaller Resistance groups merged in February 1944 into the Forces Françaises d'Intérieur (FFI, French Forces of the Interior), although the FTPF were able to keep a certain amount of autonomy. The creation of the FFI was a political success for de Gaulle as he was now the recognized leader of the French Resistance. He soon appointed Général Pierre Marie Koenig as the commander-in-chief of the FFI, although Koenig remained in London. The Allies also created the Special Projects Operations Centre (SPOC) to direct the FFI in the event of an Allied landing in southern France.

Owing to the influx of numerous Maquisards the French Resistance became a major military factor for the first time in late 1943 and early 1944, though initially only in remote areas of southern France, chiefly the Alps and the Jura. The Germans could not turn a blind eye to the potential strategic importance of this area, as the mountain passes of the Alps linked the French with the Italian theatre of war. A firm stronghold in the Alps could serve the Maquis as a launching pad for further expansion and eventually threaten the Rhône Valley, i.e. the supply artery for German forces along the French Mediterranean coast. As a result, in February 1944 the Militärbefehlshaber in Frankreich (Military Commander in France), General Carl-Heinrich von Stülpnagel, ordered the destruction of all Maquis groups over the next few weeks, i.e. before the Allies were expected to land in the west.

A *Gebirgsjäger* NCO enjoys a cigarette on Mont Janus near the Montgenèvre Pass on 1 May 1944. This photo also indicates why Maquis activity was impossible in the Alps until summer 1944; the mountains are still covered with snow. (Karl Moser)

For the first time this mission compelled the Germans to use their army against the Resistance. Previously, combating the Resistance had been purely a police task, assigned to the Sipo/SD. On 5 February 1944 the Germans launched the largest operation so far against the Maquis, Operation *Korporal*. About 2,000 soldiers from various units – amongst them companies of 157. Reserve Division – tracked down Resistance groups in the southern French Jura. Owing to heavy snowfall the operation had to be stopped prematurely on 13 February and did not succeed in destroying the Maquis in this area.

The next large operation was against the Maquis des Glières in Haute-Savoie. SOE agents had persuaded AS leaders to hold the Glières mountain plateau as a kind of natural fortress in order to demonstrate how much harm the Resistance could do to the Germans. From early February 1944 Vichy French security forces, amongst them the notorious Milice, had besieged the plateau. However, all attempts to take the stronghold failed. When *Gebirgsjäger* (mountain infantry) of 157. Reserve Division arrived in late March, the plateau was taken within two days. Many Maquisards escaped, but the plateau as such could no longer serve as a Resistance base. Two lessons could be learnt from the battle of Glières. Firstly, the weak Vichy French police forces had not been able to defeat larger Resistance groups, a fact confirmed again in April in an inconclusive operation against the Maquis du Vercors. (In future, the Germans refused to allow Vichy forces to participate in military operations against the Maquis.) Secondly, the experience from Glières should have taught the Resistance the impossibility of holding ground in a pitched battle against the Wehrmacht. However, this costly and bloody lesson was not learned and the mistake was repeated in the Vercors a few months later in July 1944.

Despite the success at Glières the French Alps were far from peaceful. Directly after the end of the operation, units of 157. Reserve Division moved again to the Jura to quell the local Maquis there. Operation *Frühling* (Spring) lasted from 7 to 18 April 1944, but, as with *Korporal* two months earlier, the Maquisards quickly dispersed. Once German troops withdrew from the area after the end of the operation the Maquisards quickly returned. Although the Germans had been able to damage the Maquis in the Jura and Alps, they were far from having defeated them.

The Allied invasion in Normandy on 6 June 1944 fundamentally changed the domestic situation in France. The Resistance mobilized and liberated a few provincial towns. Parts of southern France were in complete turmoil. However, the German response was quick and ruthless; they crushed the insurgency within a few days by brute force. The climax was the destruction of the village of Oradour-sur-Glane in central France, where a company of 2. SS-Panzer Division 'Das Reich' killed 642 inhabitants and burned down the settlement. After less than a week the insurgency collapsed in most parts of France; the Resistance had launched its military campaign too early.

The state of euphoria after 6 June also reached the Alps and the Jura. The main centre of Resistance was the mountain plateau of the Vercors, south-west of Grenoble. Here, general mobilization commenced on the night of 8–9 June; all access routes to the plateau were blocked and eventually the French Republic was declared on 3 July 1944. A large French national flag with the Gaullist Lorraine cross waved on the bluffs of the plateau, visible to the German garrison in Grenoble. The Germans could not tolerate this provocation and a general offensive against the Vercors would soon follow.

OPPOSING COMMANDERS

THE GERMANS

It is wrong to believe German military hierarchy enjoyed a coherent organization during World War II. The occupation apparatus in France and particularly in southern France constituted a classic example of the 'rule of many'. Within this 'divide-and-rule principle' there was no clear chain of command and, as a consequence, competency between or within various military and police authorities remained often vague or contradictory, often leaving room for misinterpretation between and rivalry amongst the separate factions. The following paragraphs can therefore give only a rough overview of the German occupation apparatus.

In theory the highest authority in the former 'unoccupied zone', i.e. the territory of Vichy France, was the Kommandant des Heeresgebiets Südfrankreich (Commander of the Army Area Southern France), a post held from autumn 1942 until early August 1944 by **Generalleutnant Heinrich Niehoff**. Born in 1882, Niehoff left the army after World War I and joined the Prussian police. Promoted to the rank of police major-general in 1933, he transferred to the Luftwaffe in 1936 and retired only two years later. Called back to service at the outbreak of World War II, he would never gain front-line experience during the war. Instead, he exclusively held occupation posts, initially in Lille in northern France from 1940 and then in 1942 as Commander of the Army Area Southern France in Lyon. From the few remaining records it seems Niehoff's personality was full of contradictions. On the one hand some evidence portrays him as a fairly ruthless officer who sympathized with National-Socialist ideology (in his New Year Order in early 1944 he called the French Resistance 'bandit-like sub-humanity'). On the other hand, he successfully pleaded for the release of 1,300 arrested citizens in the provincial town of Bourg-en-Bresse during the large-scale anti-partisan Operation *Treffenfeld* in early July 1944. Niehoff was in charge of the overall direction of the Vercors operation. For unknown reasons he left France in the very last days of the German occupation, and he retired from the armed forces in early August 1944.

The second most important officer involved in the Vercors operation (and to a much lesser degree the Tarentaise) was the commander of 157. Reserve Division, **Generalleutnant Karl Pflaum**. Born in Passau, Lower Bavaria, in 1890, Pflaum was an experienced field commander in both World Wars. From the outbreak of the war in 1939 until autumn 1941 he was in charge of the prestigious Infanterie Regiment 19, the traditional Bavarian regiment of the inter-war years. In autumn 1941 he assumed command of 258. Infanterie Division, but was relieved of duty during the winter crisis on the Eastern Front in January 1942 because of heart disease. His medical condition prevented him from assuming command of a front-line division again and he had to content himself with the 157. Reserve Division, a training division, in the occupied west. As a young boy Pflaum had spent some time in France and he was deemed a likeable character. Initially he also believed in waging a 'clean' war against the Maquis by avoiding reprisals against the civilian population. Over the summer months of 1944, however, his opinions seemed to have become radicalized. During the operation in the Vercors he held command only over the units of his own division. In late August 1944 Pflaum was dismissed as divisional commander, again partly because of heart problems, and partly because of his poor performance during the general German withdrawal.

The spearhead of Pflaum's 157. Reserve Division was Reserve Gebirgsjäger Regiment 1. Its commander was **Oberst Franz Schwehr**, a dubious character. By the end of World War I he held the rank of second Feldwebdleutnat, but had to leave the army and endured poverty in the 1920s. With the expansion of the Wehrmacht after 1935 he rejoined the armed forces and served as a battalion commander in France in 1940 and in Russia in 1941 where he suffered a psychological breakdown. Like his divisional commander Pflaum he was therefore no longer assessed fit for front-line duty, although he was also described as physically robust and a good mountaineer. From a tactical point of view Schwehr led his regiment with skill and success against the Maquis in spring and summer 1944. However, his attitude towards the armed Resistance and the local population was one of utmost brutality in some instances, as the events in the Tarentaise in August 1944 will show. Schwehr left his regiment in January 1945 because of illness.

Smaller operations against the Maquis would normally be directed by separate local German occupation authorities in each French department, the *Verbindungsstäbe* (Liaison Staffs). They were mostly run by older officers, colonels or major-generals, who had not excelled in their career during the war.

The commander of Verbindungsstab 735 in Grenoble, **Oberst Werner Kirsten**, seems to have socialized with the local French to the point where senior German officers of the 157. Reserve Division officially lodged a complaint about his behaviour and called him a 'trustee of the French'. In contrast, representatives of the French administration did not see it this way. The prefect for the department of Isère, Philippe Frantz, described Kirsten as a very approachable person who was always prepared to listen to the concerns of the population. Finally, Kirsten was removed from his post on 24 July 1944, only a few days after the start of the operation in the Vercors. This conflict between Kirsten and officers of the 157. Reserve Division must be seen as an example of the dilemma the Germans faced: the choice between either accommodating the French population or strict security for their own troops. With the ever-increasing danger from the Maquis, the latter option prevailed.

Running parallel to the military hierarchy was the police hierarchy, with **SS-Gruppenführer Carl Oberg** at the top as the Höherer SS- und Polizeiführer (HSSPF, Higher SS and Police Commander) in Paris. The police were responsible for imposing reprisals and for handling hostages. Subordinate to Oberg was the Befehlshaber der Sicherheitspolizei, SS-Standartenführer Helmut Knochen, with its regional branches. The Kommandeur der Sicherheitspolizei und des Sicherheitsdienstes (KdS, Commander of the Security Police and the Security Service) in Lyon, **SS-Obersturmbannführer Dr Werner Knab**, was responsible for the departments of Rhône, Ain, Haute-Savoie, Savoie, Isère, Drôme and Loire. A former law student, Knab had previously been in occupied Norway in 1940–41, but after various disagreements with his superiors he was sent to the Ukraine to 'demonstrate his reliability'. In Kiev he was made head of section IV in Einsatzgruppe C.

His areas of responsibility encompassed anti-partisan operations and the quest for 'unwanted elements' such as Jews or communists. Transferred to Lyon in autumn 1943, Knab's infamous right hand was **SS-Hauptsturmführer Klaus Barbie**, the 'butcher of Lyon'. As head of section IV, Barbie had to deal with 'enemies of the Reich', i.e. Resistance fighters and Jews. The local Sipo/SD outposts in Grenoble and Chambéry were commanded by SS-Hauptsturmführer Ludwig Heinson and Ernst Floreck respectively. All these police officers shared the same career aspirations and belief in Nazi ideology. In order to obtain the necessary information about the Resistance, they applied the most extreme measures, with torture being commonplace in German police arrest cells. After the war the French military tribunal in Lyon described Heinson as 'a perfect Nazi type and a characteristic example of a war criminal'. This statement accurately sums up the personality of most Sipo/SD men.

THE FRENCH

Whilst the Germans had to overcome disagreement, mainly between the police and the military, their French opponents also experienced similar problems. Their fault lines were manifold and ran mainly between ORA, the Gaullist AS and the communist FTPF. Establishing an underground movement with an effective hierarchy also caused friction. Southern France was divided into six different regions, named R1 to R6. The French Alps belonged to region R1 around Lyon, the 'capital of the Resistance'. Throughout the various factions and tendencies within the French Resistance it is fair to say that individual groups at departmental level and below enjoyed a great deal of autonomy. Strict command and control in a hierarchical sense was difficult to achieve in the years from 1940 to 1944. The Maquis du Vercors was the group that came closest.

The chief of staff and later head of R1 in 1943–44 was **Marcel Descour** (Resistance codename 'Bayard'), a cavalry officer. Demobilized in 1942 he immediately joined the Resistance and managed to merge the ORA and the AS in the Lyon region. After D-Day he was nominated commander of the

LEFT
The two key officers of the FFI forces in the Vercors: Colonel Marcel Descour (1899–1995) (on the left) and Lieutenant-Colonel François Huet (1905–1968) shown during a parade after liberation. Huet was in charge of the military defence of the plateau, Descour was his superior for the northern Alps region. (MRV)

RIGHT
Colonel Oronce de Galbert (1906–1990) shown to the left, during the (second) liberation of Moûtiers on 23 August 1944. Stemming from old Savoyard nobility and an officer-class family, de Galbert was the commander of the FFI forces in the departments of Savoie and Haute-Savoie. To his right is Capitaine Lungo, the commander of the FFI forces in the Upper Tarentaise. (Alain Raffain)

Alpine zone within R1 and transferred his headquarters to the Vercors, but did not interfere with the military decisions of the local commanders. His superior as head of R1 and R2, Henri Zeller ('Faisceau'), was also present in the Vercors during July 1944.

The military founder and organizer of the Resistance forces in the Vercors was **Alain Le Ray** ('Rouvier' or 'Bastide'), who had been only a first lieutenant as a *chasseur alpin* (mountain infantry) in the 159e Régiment d'Infanetrie Alpine (Alpine infantry regiment) at the outbreak of war. Taken prisoner in 1940, he was the first ever to evade the allegedly escape-proof prison camp at Colditz on 11 April 1941. Le Ray regained his home country and rejoined the French Army before he was demobilized in autumn 1942 with its dissolution. A prolific and talented mountaineer, the Parisian Le Ray combined charisma, organizational skills and selfless commitment to liberating his country from the occupiers and setting up the Maquis du Vercors. In early 1944, however, he left the Vercors after a dispute with Descour. Instead he became *chef départemental* in Isère for the FFI forces and organized other Maquis groups in the area.

Le Ray's successor was **François Huet** ('Hervieux'). Born in 1905 and stemming from an officer-class family, he passed the elite French officers' school St Cyr in 1925–26 and joined the colonial troops. A highly intelligent man. he absorbed the idea – widely held within the colonial army – that an officer should not concentrate purely on his military profession, but should also play a social role in France and the empire. After the disastrous campaign in 1940 Huet was accepted into the Vichy army, but after its dissolution in November 1942 he joined the Resistance and went underground early in 1944. In May 1944 he was appointed military leader of the Maquis du Vercors. After the war Huet was often blamed for being mainly responsible for the tragedy of the French Resistance forces on the plateau. His critics claimed he had not grasped the requirements of waging a guerrilla war and had instead stuck too close to conventional warfare. This debate has not taken full account of the difficult situation Huet found himself in; he had to accommodate the various factions and political views of the Resistance forces on the plateau, a task which proved nigh-on impossible.

As the Vercors was officially declared a republic on 3 July 1944 it had a president: **Eugène Chavant** ('Clément'), a local socialist politician and NCO veteran from the Great War. He had opposed the foreign occupation of his home country from the beginning, abandoned his mayoral post in the small town of Saint-Martin-d'Hères in Isère and had gone underground. Considered a headstrong character, Chavant did not shy away from expressing his views. In the critical days of the German attack on the plateau, Chavant mostly bowed down to the military, although he had some serious issues with some of them, especially Capitaine Narcisse Geyer ('Thivollet'), the commander of the FFI forces in the south of the plateau. In addition, Yves Farge, the Commissar of the Republic in the Lyon area, had made frequent visits to the Vercors before the battle.

Le Ray's military counterpart in Savoie was Oronce de Galbert ('Mathieu'), who took up responsibility for the FFI forces in the two *départements* Haute-Savoie and Savoie from 6 June 1944. As with many other Resistance leaders in this area de Galbert hailed from the French officers' corps of the inter-war years and graduated from St Cyr in 1926. His right hand and most active subordinate during his time in the Resistance was **Jean Bulle** ('Devèze' or 'Baffert') a young man of 30 in 1944. Also a St Cyrien, he joined the *chasseurs alpins* (after some time in the infantry) and distinguished himself by his bravery in June 1940 on the Franco-Italian front. After the dissolution of the French Army in November 1942 he went underground and became one of the most charismatic personalities in the Resistance movement in that area. Displaying great organizational skills he managed his FFI battalion effectively from a military point of view. After the short-lived liberation of the Tarentaise Valley, Bulle was trying to negotiate the surrender of the German garrison in Albertville when he was taken prisoner and shot on 22 August 1944 on the personal order of Oberst Schwehr.

In short, the vast majority of the key military leaders in the Vercors and Savoie were formerly professional French Army officers. Mostly born between 1905 and 1913, they were too young to have fought in the Great War. Very few had combat experience in the conflict in the colonies during the inter-war years and some of them saw only sporadic fighting in 1939–40. When joining the Resistance, quite a number of them had to overcome some of their convictions in order to fight as guerrilla commanders rather than as officers in the regular French Army. Above all, joining the Maquis meant a life of constant danger. Bulle summarized it with the following words: 'I left everything for my new colleagues: family, love, the easy life. If the Germans capture me alive, I will be shot. And shot in the back like the officers of the Armée Secrète. But I have always dreamt of falling like the St Cyriens in 1914: with panache and white gloves.'

OPPOSING ARMIES

THE GERMANS

In the fifth year of the war the strain on German manpower could be felt everywhere in occupied France. The high rate of losses on the Eastern Front had taken its toll on the occupation forces in France, resulting in a mishmash of various units. The genuine occupation troops were the *Landesschützenbataillone* or *Sicherungsbataillone* (Territorial or Security Battalions), units formed of elder family fathers in their 30s or 'last sons'. In the northern Alps, Sicherungs Regiment 200 and Landesschützen Bataillon 685 were supposed to guard railway lines, depots, bridges, etc. In addition, one battalion of SS-Polizei Regiment 19 was deployed in Annecy and another one later in Lyon. The occupation troops also included *Ostbataillone* (eastern battalions). These units had been raised from ex-Red Army soldiers in 1942–43 to fight in the Soviet Union, but after mass desertions in 1943 Hitler decided to send these troops to the occupied west. Often called 'Mongols' by the local French, the *Ostbataillone* soon gained a horrible reputation for looting, raping and various other misdeeds. However they were also prone to desertion to the Maquis. In the Vercors, eastern battalions mainly

A group of 17- and 18-year-old *Gebirgsjäger* recruits leave from Munich Central Station to go to France, spring 1944. The *Gebirgsjäger* of 157. Reserve Division recruited mainly from Southern Bavaria, but also took volunteers from the rest of Germany. (Heinrich Henning)

NCO instructors of 1. Kompanie/Reserve Gebirgjsäger Bataillon 99. All of them are combat-experienced veterans from the Eastern Front wearing the Iron Cross and the Infantry Assault Badge on their tunics. (Karl Moser)

from the Freiwilligen Stamm Regiment 3 were used both for the encirclement and for the general attack on the plateau, where they spread fear and terror amongst the Maquis and the civilian population. In addition, Ostbataillon 406 guarded the important railway line between Grenoble and the French–Italian border through the Isère and Maurienne valleys.

All the above-mentioned units were regarded as third class from a military point of view. They lacked armament and their soldiers often lacked the training and the physical condition to track down the Maquis in strenuous operations in mountainous terrain. They would serve well enough for encirclement duties, but offensive actions mainly had to be carried out by other troops. In the Alps this task was entrusted to the 157. Reserve Division. Actually a training division for young recruits, it transferred from Munich to the French Jura in autumn 1942 and later, with the capitulation of the Italian forces in September 1943, to the Alps in the area around Grenoble. The 157. Reserve Division received young recruits mainly from Southern Bavaria who had just passed their basic military training. After half a year of intense further training in the division the young soldiers were finally transferred to the field army.

The division's cadre was formed of officers and NCOs with combat experience from the 1939–40 campaigns and the Eastern Front. However, owing to previous injuries the vast majority of them were no longer deemed fit for front-line duties, at least on the Eastern Front. Most officers, and particularly infantry officers, held military decorations such as the Iron Cross or the Infantry Assault Badge. However, only very few of them had been awarded higher medals and no one had been decorated with the highest German military decoration, the Knight's Cross. The division could certainly rely on some talented and skilful officers and NCOs, but overall the cadre was far from first class.

In summer 1944 157. Reserve Division consisted of two infantry regiments (Reserve Gebirgsjäger Regiment 1 and Reserve Grenadier Regiment 157), an artillery regiment (Reserve Artillerie Regiment 7), an engineer battalion (Reserve Pionier Bataillon 7) and various divisional units (signals, logistics etc). The division's most powerful formation was doubtlessly Reserve Gebirgsjäger Regiment 1 commanded by Oberst Franz Schwehr. It was an unusually large regiment, with four battalions plus a signals and mountain anti-tank company. Each mountain infantry battalion was formed of four companies, amongst them two *Jäger* (light infantry) companies, one machine-gun company and one heavy company, the latter ones normally being split up on operations. The most powerful assets were certainly the two infantry support guns (7.5cm leichtes Infanteriegeschütz 18) in each battalion. Furthermore, the battalions were armed with medium and light mortars. MG34s and even captured Italian machine guns, the outdated and rather poorly performing Breda 30 (German designation: leichtes MG099), were standard.

German occupation troops

Kommandant Heeresgebiet Südfrankreich (Commander Army Area Southern France)
Generalleutnant Heinrich Niehoff, from early August: General Ernst Dehner

157. Reserve Division
Generalleutnant Karl Pflaum

    Kommandeur der Divisions Nachschuptruppen 1057: Major Franz Werdlich

    Reserve Nachrichten Kompanie 7

    Reserve Gebirgsjäger Regiment 1: Oberst Franz Schwehr

        Reserve Gebirgs Nachrichten Kompanie 1

        Reserve Gebirgs Panzerjäger Kompanie 1

        Reserve Gebirgsjäger Bataillon I/98: Hauptmann Ludwig Stöckl

        Reserve Gebirgsjäger Bataillon II/98: Hauptmann Rudolf Geyer, from mid-July: Hauptmann Clemens Rességuier de Miremont

        Reserve Gebirgsjäger Bataillon 99: Hauptmann Hans Schneider (probably only until June)

        Reserve Gebirgsjäger Bataillon 100: Hauptmann Johann Kunstmann

    Reserve Grenadier Regiment 157: Oberstleutnant Maximilian Kneitinger

        Reserve Infanterie Geschütz Kompanie 7

        Reserve Infanterie Geschütz Kompanie 157

        Reserve Infanterie Panzerjäger Kompanie 7

        Reserve Infanterie Panzerjäger Kompanie 157

        Reserve Infanterie Pionier Kompanie 7

        Reserve Infanterie Nachrichten Kompanie 157

        Reserve Grenadier Bataillon 179: Major Johann Kolb, from early August Hauptmann Hans Obser

        Reserve Grenadier Bataillon 217: Major Georg Raith

    Reserve Artillerie Regiment 7: Oberst Alfred Seeger

        Reserve Artillerie Abteilung 7: Major Johannes Schlegel

        Reserve Gebirgs Artillerie Abteilung 79: Major Kurt Hagl

    Reserve Pionier Bataillon 7: Major Hans Rudeloff

Sicherungs Regiment 200 (4 battalions): Oberstleutnant Rudolf Ufer
Landesschützenbataillon 685: commander unknown
Ostbatallion 406: Major Bernhard Werner
Ostbatallion (Turk) 781 (only in August): commander unknown

SS-Polizei Regiment 19: SS-Obersturmbannführer Hubert Kölblinger

    I Bataillon: SS-Sturbannführer Richard Maiwald

    III Bataillon (from July): SS-Hauptsturmführer Otremba

Freiwilligen Stamm Division: Generalmajor Wilhelm von Henning

    Freiwilligen Stamm Regiment 3: Major Wilhelm Sebald, from July: Major Anton Werner

German occupation and administration troops in the Rhône-Alpes region, summer 1944

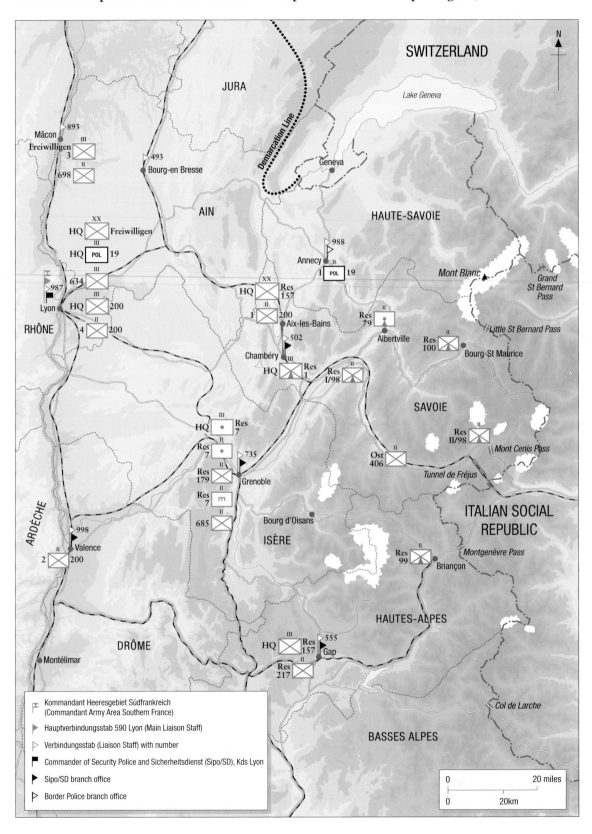

The second infantry regiment, Reserve Grenadier Regiment 157 (commander: Oberstleutnant Maximilian Kneitinger), was of a much lower standard than its partner, Reserve Gebirgsjäger Regiment 1, as it had to integrate many non-German soldiers from the annexed territories and numbered only two battalions with three companies each. Reserve Artillerie Regiment 7, commanded by Oberst Alfred Seeger, was also a very weak formation with only two battalions at two batteries each, one heavy and one light, with 15 guns overall.

For the operation in the Vercors the Germans deployed two additional formations: Kampfgruppe Zabel and Kampfgruppe Schäfer. The former consisted of a reinforced *Panzergrenadier* (armoured infantry) battalion with the strength of about 800 men from Panzergrenadier Regiment 10 (9. Panzer Division). It had been formed as a quick-reaction force just after D-Day to quell the Maquis in the Rhône Valley and had seen major action around Valréas (Vaucluse) and Privas (Ardèche) in June 1944. Major Zabel did not take over command of the battlegroup from Major Heinz Unger until mid-July. For the Vercors operation Marschbataillon Müller from 352. Infanterie Division was attached to Kampfgruppe Zabel. Nothing else is known about this unit.

A new departure for anti-partisan operations in France was the deployment of airborne forces. In the Vercors two parachute companies were to land in the heart of the plateau. Kampfgruppe Schäfer was designated for special operations as 7. Kompanie of Kampfgeschwader 200. The unit recruited soldiers with a history of poor discipline and the operation against the Maquis would allow them to undertake a kind of probation. In the weeks before, the soldiers underwent hard physical and psychological training with strict selection criteria. The paratroopers' armament was confined to small arms, notably the MG42, and light mortars, but they could count on support from the skies. The Luftwaffe would play a crucial role in defeating the Maquis on the plateau in a transport, supply, rescue or close air support role. The last of these was provided by Geschwader Bongart, a formation which campaigned against the FFI in Southern France all summer. By late June it numbered 67 planes (36 combat-ready) of various types, mostly the old-fashioned Italian Re 2002 fighter bomber. Overall the Germans mustered about 8,000 to 10,000 men in the Vercors and probably 1,500 in the Tarentaise.

The Germans acquired all their intelligence through the channels of the Sipo/SD with its local branches in each department's capital. Those branches were, however, very small in number. The SD in Chambéry for instance numbered barely 13 men! In addition, however, the Sipo/SD had a vast and effective agent network. It was able, on 8–9 June during the mobilization of the Maquis du Vercors, to infiltrate it by employing a number of informers who proved to be invaluable sources of information. Sipo/SD officers and NCOs were assigned to Wehrmacht units in most of the anti-partisan operations in the French Alps and were partly responsible for the execution of reprisals and the handling of suspects. However, the relationship between the two institutions was not particularly good. There was a fair amount of friction between the infamous Knab, Barbie and their colleagues and the officers of 157. Reserve Division, who wanted to act more moderately on some occasions, particularly towards the innocent French population. Furthermore, the Wehrmacht did not regard the policemen as military professionals and therefore did not want to concede them any powers in military operations.

The Germans did not use the French only as agents, but also in a combat role, albeit in a very limited way. Confirmed collaborators were recruited into the 8. Kompanie/Brandenburg Regiment 2, a small unit specializing in anti-partisan operations and often behaving with utmost ruthlessness. It is likely that some French collaborators from the Brandenburg Regiment landed on the Vercors plateau with Kampfgruppe Schäfer. Vichy's police and paramilitary forces, such as the Groupes Mobiles de Réserve (GMR) and the Milice, did not really have any influence, either in the Vercors or in the Tarentaise. After their failure at Glières in spring 1944 the Germans used the Milice only for minor auxiliary tasks and declined the GMR's services altogether.

THE FRENCH

The French Resistance did not exist as a coherent organization during the occupation; it was more of an amalgamation of different factions. The formation of the FFI in February 1944 meant at least some unity of command. Owing to the influx of former professional officers and the ORA–AS merger in the French Alps, most local Resistance leaders were keen to form their men into some kind of military organization as soon as possible. This was particularly evident in the Vercors. The Resistance forces were to mirror a regular army in order to gain legitimacy in the eyes of the French population and legality in the eyes of the Germans. They did not achieve the latter; after some lengthy internal discussions about the legal status of the French insurgents, the German Supreme Commander West decided to deny combatant status to all Resistance forces in

One of the early Maquis groups in the Vercors, August 1943. At this stage the young Maquisards were not yet armed Resistance fighters, but had just escaped the STO (compulsory labour service) and were often recklessly adventurous and indulged in a life of illegal activity. (MRV)

June 1944. Prisoners were therefore mostly shot on the spot or in some cases deported to Germany for forced labour.

The history of the Maquis du Vercors commenced at the end of the winter of 1942–43 when the first men gathered on the plateau to escape from the Italian–German occupation and set up camp. By the end of 1943 most men on the plateau were between 18 and 23 years of age with just less than half of them coming from the immediate local area. A large number of these men just wanted to escape compulsory labour service, the STO, and initially had no intention of taking up arms. Alain Le Ray proved to be the right man to mould these men into some kind of military force, although they were only very poorly armed. Caches from the old, disbanded French Army, booty from the Italians in autumn 1943 and in particular Allied container drops increased the Maquis's armament, but weapons generally remained a key issue for the Maquisards. Moreover, food was often difficult to obtain and had to be organized from the local farmers, either by voluntary contribution or sometimes by force. The transformation of the Maquis du Vercors into a fighting force also meant changing its political allegiance. Initially rather socialist, it soon became predominantly Gaullist with the arrival of former army officers.

BELOW LEFT
On 25 June 1944 FFI parade in St Martin-en-Vercors. The 11e Régiment de Cuirassiers hoists the Tricolour with its commander Capitaine Narcisse Geyer on his horse with sabre drawn. (MRV)

BELOW RIGHT
Capitaine Louis Fayard (right) inspects men of the 14e BCA in the Forêt de Lente. In this battalion and the 12e BCA the influence of ex-military personnel was relatively low; both battalions played only a minor role during the fighting in July 1944. (MRV)

The Maquis du Vercors became fully operational and achieved general mobilization on 8–9 June 1944. A huge influx of enthusiastic young volunteers boosted the number of fighters considerably; overall, around 4,000 men gathered on the plateau. The food problem could be solved thanks to the local farmers' mostly cooperative attitude; the problem of obtaining arms, however, still remained. Though there were a number of Bren guns and PIATs, not all men on the plateau could be issued with small arms. Despite three requests between general mobilization on 8–9 June and the German attack on 21 July, the Allies did not drop any heavy weapons such as field guns or mortars, as they considered these weapons useless in guerrilla warfare. The Maquis du Vercors possessed only one captured German anti-tank gun – but even that lacked a sight.

Huet endeavoured to make the Maquis appear a legitimate force and organized his own headquarters in a strictly military sense. He also ordered restoring the former regional French regiments. Therefore, the 11e Régiment de Cuirassiers, the 6e, 12e and 14e Bataillons de Chasseurs Alpins (BCA), the 4e Régiment de Genie as well as the 2e Régiment d'Artillerie were resurrected. This was not merely symbolic, but also an attempt to instill military discipline into the men. Yet, all this could not conceal the lack of trained cadres. The Maquis du Vercors numbered only 169 former regular officers and 317 NCOs. The large majority of the fighters were young and inexperienced men. The few French and Allied instructors tried everything to train them fully but, owing to shortage of time and ammunition, this task turned out to be too challenging.

The reconstitution of the old regiments also meant that the old Maquis designations in individual camps became obsolete. Many Maquisards who had been on the plateau for months disliked the 'militarization' of their Maquis. Some of the tensions between former military men and 'civilian' Maquisards could never be fully redressed – in particular with regard to the commander of the 11e Cuirassiers, Capitaine Narcisse Geyer, whose elitist bearing as a cavalry officer met disapproval amongst the veteran Maquisards.

The FFI in Savoie experienced in many ways the same problems as their colleagues in the Vercors: a deficit of instructors and no heavy weapons. At least the general lack of small arms was finally resolved with the container drop on 1 August at the Col de Saisies, the largest of its kind during the occupation. This drop allowed the entire area to be armed; in the Tarentaise alone armed Maquisards numbered around 1,300 (1,000 AS and 320 FTPF). However, their lack of training, combined with patriotic enthusiasm, often did more harm than good. There was always an underlying danger that the Maquisards tended to throw themselves prematurely into action and as a result suffered unnecessary casualties. In the Savoie the Resistance faced another problem so typical for France during these months and weeks: the rift between the communist FTPF and the Gaullist AS within the FFI forces. This problem would have a disastrous impact on the operational plan in the Tarentaise.

THE ALLIES: BRITISH AND US INVOLVEMENT

Allied support for the French Resistance took many forms: container drops with arms and supply, liaison officers and training teams such as the tripartite three-men 'Jedburghs' or the Operational Groups (OGs) of the US Army. Eight Jedburgh Teams operated in the northern parts of the French Alps; three of them dropped in June and helped in one way or another to train Maquisards in the Vercors area. Another five Jedburgh Teams did not arrive in the wider region until August, when it was virtually too late to achieve anything tangible. The most important military reinforcement for the Maquis du Vercors was the 15-man-strong OG 'Justine' under the command of Captain Vernon G. Hoppers. The men, dropped during the night of 28–29 June near Vassieux-en-Vercors, carried out guerrilla actions against German supply and communications lines, and helped to instruct the French Resistance fighters in the use of British and US weapons. Two other OGs were dispatched to this region, but far too late and thus with rather inconclusive results. Each OG consisted of two officers and 13 NCOs, all highly trained French-speaking volunteers.

The Allies also sent liaison missions, called Inter-Allied Missions, into France. They had to establish contact with the local Resistance, advise them, and enable them to forward their wishes and requests to London or Algiers. Under no circumstances, however, were the Inter-Allied Missions to assume command over Maquis groups. These should remain firmly in the hands of the local French leaders. In late 1943 Mission 'Union I' operated in the Savoie, Isère and Ain regions; upon return to London in spring 1944 the mission members praised the high potential for guerrilla action. In additon, SOE Major Francis Cammaerts ('Roger'), a half-Belgian who spoke fluent French operated in the area from 1943 and set up a huge agent network ('Jockey'); however, he sometimes tried to pursue his own personal policy. In spring 1944, the SOE officially appointed Cammaerts as head of all Allied missions in south-eastern France.

During summer 1944 two Inter-Allied Missions were dispatched to the French Alps: 'Eucalyptus' on 28–29 June to the Vercors and 'Union II' on 1 August to Savoie. The commander of 'Eucalyptus' was Major Desmond Longe ('Refraction') accompanied by his second in command, Captain (later Major) John Houseman ('Reflexion'), the American First Lieutenant André Pecquet ('Paray') and another three Frenchmen. The two British officers, both from the Norfolk Regiment, were a rather doubtful choice for this critical mission in the Vercors. Neither of them really spoke French and all communication in the meetings with Huet and the other leaders had to be done via translators, usually Pecquet. Longe, a banker, had at least travelled in Latin America before the war, but Houseman, a land agent and surveyor from High Wycombe, had never left the UK before. In all seriousness, in his SOE questionnaire he named the Home Counties as his geographical area of expertise. At least in dealing with the Resistance leaders, both men displayed social and diplomatic skills, but overall 'Eucalyptus' was of very limited help to the Maquis du Vercors. Besides, the mission had to overcome some friction with Major Cammaerts whom they considered too selfish.

In contrast to 'Eucalyptus' the personnel for 'Union II' were well chosen. The commander was Major Peter J. Ortiz ('Chambellan'), who had already been in the Alps area with the 'Union I' Mission in 1943–44. A quarter French he was fluent in seven languages and had spent some years in the French Foreign Legion in the 1930s. Ortiz and his seven men parachuted into Savoie on 1 August 1944, together with the large container drop at the Col de Saisies. What distinguished Ortiz and another five men of 'Union II' from all other US armed personnel in the European theatre of war was their branch: they belonged to the US Marine Corps (USMC). These were the only Marines deployed in Europe during World War II, even though 'Union II' was not a specific USMC unit, as it also contained a British and a French officer.

OPPOSING PLANS

THE GERMANS

From 1941 the German Army had accumulated a good deal of experience in fighting irregulars on the Eastern Front and the Balkans. However, their level of expertise was fairly low. The underlying political problem was never really addressed: a discontented populace in the occupied territories who often feared for their own lives. Constrained by their Nazi ideology the Germans could not or would not tackle the political issues, although there was no shortage of Wehrmacht commanders who raised their voices in warning. German rule was marked by oppression, although to differing degrees, in the various occupied countries.

The Germans contented themselves with improving their tactics for eliminating the partisan threat and developed some relatively imaginative approaches from a purely military point of view. On a local level they operated in platoon strength with flexible *Jagdkommandos* (hunting detachments), copying partisan tactics based on the element of surprise. On a regional level the Germans carried out large-scale operations. In the east or the Balkans these operations could include up to several divisions. That scale was never reached in France where only a few thousand men from various units and formations were deployed at maximum at one time.

The 157. Reserve-Division was the formation with most expertise in fighting the partisans in France. From autumn 1943 its units had been deployed again and again in various large-scale operations in the Alps and the French Jura. Mostly these operations followed a similar approach; the 'infested' area was first encircled along natural barriers or main roads, then a number of *Kampfgruppen* thrust into enemy territory. Any partisans trying to flee would have been caught at the ring of encirclement if not sooner. Owing to a constant lack of troops, however, this ring could never be as tight as the Germans wished. The most successful operation of this kind took place on the Plateau de Glières in late March 1944 where 157. Reserve Division's mountain infantry annihilated the local Maquis. Glières would serve as a blueprint for later operations in Alpine terrain such as the Vercors.

Therefore, in the Vercors the Germans planned to encircle the enemy forces on the plateau by occupying the low ground along the Isère River in the north and various regional roads to the west. The troops for the encirclement came mainly from Reserve Grenadier Regiment 157, of which Reserve Grenadier Bataillon 179 guarded the northern part of the ring and

Maquis in the R1 sector and major German anti-partisan operations in 1944

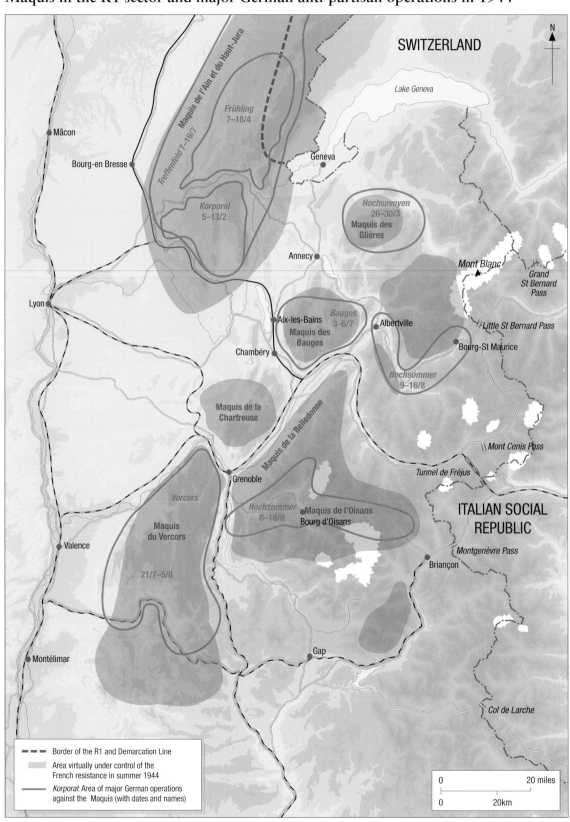

SWITZERLAND

Mâcon

Bourg-en Bresse

Maquis de l'Ain et du Haut-Jura

Treffenfeld 7–19/7

Frühling 7–18/4

Lake Geneva

Geneva

Korporal 5–13/2

Hochsavoyen 26–30/3
Maquis des Glières

Annecy

Lyon

Mont Blanc

Grand St Bernard Pass

Aix-les-Bains
Maquis des Bauges

Bauges 3–6/7

Albertville

Little St Bernard Pass

Chambéry

Bourg-St Maurice

Hochsómmer 9–16/8

Maquis de la Chartreuse

Maquis de la Belledonne

Mont Cenis Pass

Tunnel de Fréjus

Grenoble

Vercors

Hochsommer 8–18/8

Maquis de l'Oisans
Bourg d'Oisans

ITALIAN SOCIAL REPUBLIC

Maquis du Vercors

Montgenèvre Pass

Valence

Briançon

21/7–5/8

Montélimar

Gap

Col de Larche

N

- - - Border of the R1 and Demarcation Line

Area virtually under control of the French resistance in summer 1944

Korporal: Area of major German operations against the Maquis (with dates and names)

0   20 miles

0   20km

Reserve Grenadier Bataillon 217, along with some additional companies, closed the gap around the Col de la Haute Croix in the south-east. To the west a mix of various other units completed the ring of encirclement: three battalions of eastern troops from the Freiwilligen Stamm Regiment 3, elements of SS-Polizei Regiment 19, a reinforced battalion of Sicherungs Regiment 200 and 200 men of the *Feldgendarmerie*, the Army police. Yet, all these troops played only a secondary role in this operation.

Major German anti-partisan operations in the Alps and the Jura in 1944				
Codename	Area	Dates	Strength and units involved	Results
Korporal	Southern French Jura	5–13 Feb 1944	c.2,000 men from ResGebJg Bn I/98, elements of 272. Inf Div, 2. Bn/Sicherungs Regt 194, elements of Sicherungs Regt 200, Sipo/SD, elements of Polizei Regt 'Todt'	Maquis disperses quickly; operation finally cancelled owing to heavy snowfall
Hoch-Savoyen	Plateau de Glières	26–30 Mar 1944	c.3,000 men from ResGebJg Regt 1 and smaller detachments of 157. ResDiv, French Milice, Sipo/SD	Maquis stronghold destroyed; operation seen by the Germans as a blueprint for mountain operations against the Maquis
Frühling	Central French Jura	7–18 Apr 1944	c.3,000 men from ResGebJg Regt 1 and smaller detachments of 157. ResDiv, Sipo/SD	Maquis disperses quickly and cannot be destroyed
Bauges	Massif de Bauges	3–6 Jul 1944	c.3,500 men from ResGebJg Regt 1 and smaller detachments of 157. ResDiv, elements of SS-Polizei Regiment 19, Sipo/SD	Maquis disrupted, but can avoid destruction through dispersal
Treffenfeld	Southern and central French Jura	7–19 Jul 1944	c.5,000–6,000 men from ResGebJg Regt 1, various eastern troops (amongst them Cossacks), Officers School Dijon, Luftwaffe ground units, French Milice, Sipo/SD	Maquis disperses quickly and avoids destruction in the Jura for a third time
Vercors/ Bettina	Massif du Vercors	21 Jul–5 Aug 1944	c.8,000–10,000 men from almost all units of 157. ResDiv, 7. Coy Kampfgeschwader 200, 2. Bn/Panzergrenadier Regt 10, elements of SS-Polizei Regt 19 and Sicherungs Regt 200, various eastern troops, substantial air support by Kampfgeschwader Bongart, Sipo/SD	Maquis stronghold destroyed, but vast majority of Maquisards able to escape; extensive reprisals against the civilian population
Hochsommer (Phase 1)	Romanche Valley	8–18 Aug 1944	c.3,000–4,000 men from various units of 157. ResDiv, Ost Bn 781, Sipo/SD	Maquis disperses; planned deportation of male civilian population and raw materials from this area has to be given up owing to lack of transport
Hochsommer (Phase 2)	Tarentaise	10–16 Aug 1944	c.1,500–2,000 men from ResGbJg Bn 100, ResGren Bn 179, 79. ResMountain Arty Bn 79 and 2. Bn/SS-Polizei Regt 15	Maquis heavily disrupted, but major elements able to escape into the high mountains; valley passable again for the Germans

The actual attack was to be carried out by four different *Kampfgruppen*. To the south-west the *Panzergrenadiere* of Kampfgruppe Zabel with elements of an unknown eastern battalion pushed eastwards along the river Drôme; in the original plan they were only supposed to close the encirclement of the plateau in the south at the town of Die. the other three *Kampfgruppen* were to launch the attack onto the plateau. To the north-east lay the only actual weak spot in the natural defences of the Vercors. This was the sector where Kampfgruppe Seeger attacked with two reserve *Gebirgsjäger* battalions (99 and 100) supported by engineers and artillery. The really daring missions had to be carried out by the two remaining *Kampfgruppen*: Kampfgruppe Schwehr and Kampfgruppe Schäfer. Experienced in operations against the Maquis, Oberst Schwehr was tasked with taking the steep, narrow and remote mountain passes to the south-east of the plateau, i.e. at a point where nobody expected the Germans to attack and hence where French positions were undermanned. Kampfgruppe Schwehr was formed by two reserve *Gebirgsjäger* battalions (I/98 and II/98) with half a company, i.e. two guns of Reserve Gebirgs Artillerie Abteilung 79.

A new departure for anti-partisan operations in France was the deployment of airborne units. Two companies of Kampfgruppe Schäfer were to land in the heart of the plateau around the village of Vassieux-en-Vercors. This was where the Germans wrongly assumed the Maquis's HQ to be, which in reality was located in St Martin-en-Vercors. After taking Vassieux, Kampfgruppe Schäfer would march towards La Chapelle-en-Vercors and St Agnan-en-Vercors. Furthermore, the *Kampfgruppe* was to be reinforced from the air by eastern troops and Brandenburgers before they would finally be relieved by troops of Kampfgruppe Schwehr. From Chabeuil airfield near Valence fighter-bombers of Kampfgeschwader Bongart would provide close air support for the ground troops, and transport aircraft from

German *Fallschirmjäger* practice the rapid exit of troops from a DFS 230. The Germans still used this glider for smaller airborne commando-style operations, such as those in the Vercors, even following the battle for Crete in May 1941. (BA, 101I-569-1579-14A)

Luftlandegeschwader (LLG, Airborne Wing) 1 and 2 were to supply the airborne elements at Vassieux. All four *Kampfgruppen* had Sipo/SD personnel attached for the interrogation of prisoners and suspects; these men would also advise on or order reprisals. After the operation started this plan had to be adapted slightly to the tactcial situation, in particular with regard to the role of Kampfgruppen Zable and Schäfer.

The offensive in the Tarentaise (Operation *Hochsommer*), which followed the operation in the Vercors was a classic fight-through operation in a mountain valley. The isolated garrison from Bourg-St-Maurice which had withdrawn to the Little St Bernard Pass had to be relieved. German forces were composed of Reserve Gebirgsjäger Bataillon 100, Reserve Grenadier Bataillon 179 and elements of Reserve Gebirgs Artillerie Abteilung 79. The troops started at Albertville and advanced along the sometimes extremely narrow Tarentaise Valley. Any opposition they met was to be outflanked by mountain infantry on the adjacent slopes and finally German forces should envelop the enemy forces in the valley. How to defeat the Resistance fighters farther up the mountains remained, however, an open question. Air support was only very limited.

Oberleutnant Friedrich Schäfer (1919–1992), the commander of the airborne forces which landed at Vassieux on 21 July 1944. The Knight's Cross reveals this photo was taken after the operation. Schäfer was the only German awarded this prestigious military medal for anti-partisan operations in France during World War II. (BA, 146-2006-0089)

Finally, it is important to mention that German operations were constantly accompanied by harsh reprisals against the local population. Selective terrorization in the form of shooting hostages or burning down houses was key to German anti-partisan warfare. In theory, the Germans were not to lash out blindly against the entire population, but try to target supporters of the partisans instead. Very often this worked well, owing to the Sipo/SD's relatively effective network of agents. In a large number of instances, however, innocent people were killed too. The German officer responsible would not expect to undergo disciplinary action, since a central order from Supreme Commander West – the Sperrle-Erlass, dated 3 February 1944 – had sanctioned the misconduct of troops on anti-partisan operations.

THE FRENCH

Central to French planning in the Vercors was the *Plan Montagnard* (Mountain Plan). Its 'father' was Pierre Dalloz, a passionate mountaineer, who drafted the *Paper on the Military Possibilities of the Vercors* in December 1942. The Vercors plateau, 45km in length and 20km in width, would serve as a natural fortress against any penetration from the occupying forces. The paper was vague on many points; it distinguished between an 'Immediate Action Programme', with the establishment of landing zones, and a 'Further Action Programme', with the Vercors becoming an offensive base in the event of an Allied landing in southern France. Dalloz discussed his plan with the principal leaders of the Gaullist Resistance movement: Yves Farge, Jean Moulin and Général Delestraint. The latter took the project to London in February 1943 and the Free French in exile approved it. *Montagnard* was to go ahead and receive substantial financial and material backing. Unfortunately, the Germans arrested Moulin and Delestraint in June 1943; as a consequence the personal link between *Montagnard* in France and the Free French in London was broken.

Original German plan for the attack against the Maquis du Vercors

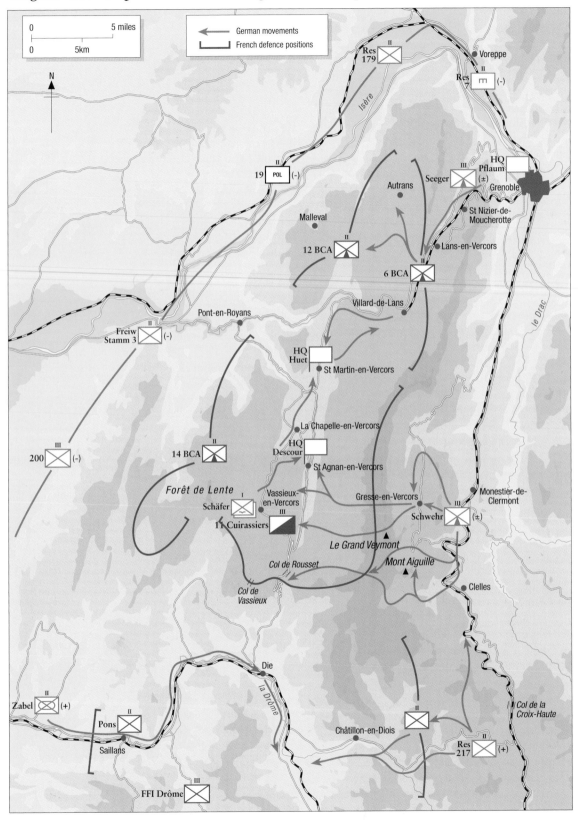

All future planning in France for *Montagnard* was now based on the false assumption that the Free French and the Allies would wholeheartedly support it. In reality, *Montagnard* was no longer given consideration in London and this tragic misunderstanding would have disastrous consequences for the fight in July 1944. Dalloz was wholly unaware of this fundamental change in the situation and proceeded with his project by drafting an even more ambitious plan in late 1943, together with Alain Le Ray, the military commander of the Vercors. The mountain massif was to become a safe haven for the Maquis and at the same time a springboard for offensive operations against the German lines of communication in the wider region. *Montagnard* was not solely about holding ground, but also about penetrating enemy terrain in all directions.

In his plan Le Ray divided the Vercors into five sub-sectors with three command posts each. He assumed he would need about 8,000 armed men for his plan to succeed. Apart from the demolition of routes and bridges, 800 machine guns and in particular 15 mortars and 5 anti-tank guns were deemed crucial to the entire plan, in order to deny the enemy access to the interior of the plateau. The heavy weapons were to be mainly deployed in the area around St Nizier, i.e. the weakest point of the 'natural fortress'. In reality, however, the Maquisards would never receive those heavy weapons. A basic military asset was therefore missing in a plan that seemed to be brilliant at first glance. Le Ray hoped to hold the plateau for four to five days against the German forces. *Montagnard* remained the operational plan for the Maquis, even after Le Ray's departure. Fantastic ideas circulated in the heads of some French planners, such as the landing of an entire airborne division on the plateau.

Alain Le Ray (1910–2007) was a key leader of the Resistance in the Alps. He was responsible for the military aspect of the ill-fated *Plan Montagnard*. He was also the first military commander in the Vercors, after which he became commander of the FFI forces in Isère in spring 1944. (UTM)

It would be wrong to regard *Montagnard* in the same light as the passive and defensive Maginot attitude held by the French officer corps during the inter-war years. Whilst the French Army in 1939–40 displayed an astonishing resistance towards any form of offensive thinking, *Montagnard* was at least in theory an offensive plan. Carried out in strict cooperation with the Allied landings in southern France it would indeed have created great opportunities. In reality, however, it lacked the manpower, the armament, the training and above all the necessary support from the Allies to succeed. Yet the commanding officers on the plateau, especially Huet, stuck to a plan whose basic requirements just did not exist and tried to fight a pitched battle.

The French plan for the Tarentaise contained the same recipe for disaster as that in the Vercors; after liberating a particular area, the FFI hoped to hold the ground or at least to delay considerably any enemy advance until Allied reinforcements arrived. However, it was unclear how those reinforcements were to reach the liberated areas and join up with the FFI; this crucial question was seemingly never discussed. At least, in Savoie the Maquis had a contingency plan; if the worst came to the worst, they could return to the inaccessible mountains and the neighbouring valleys. The Beaufortain in particular, to the north of the Tarentaise, always remained a safe haven for the FFI as all smaller German attacks there had previously failed.

In fairness it must be stressed that not all Resistance forces in the Alps believed in their ability to hold ground. For example, the legendary Compagnie Stéphane, which operated in the area to the east of Grenoble, under its charismatic leader Etienne Poitou Stéphane, a young former regular officer in the *chasseurs alpins*. The first principle for his small elite force was to be always on the move like 'nomads' and to avoid becoming stationary at all costs. This played to the strengths of the guerrillas and minimized the enemy's superior firepower. The second principle was to keep contact with the civilian population to the absolute minimum. This resulted in reducing the risk of betrayal on the one hand and lessening the exposure of civilians to German reprisals on the other. Although Compagnie Stéphane carried out some successful ambushes on German columns, it should be noted that in the wider military sense it did not achieve very much.

THE BATTLE FOR THE VERCORS

THE BUILD-UP PHASE

The general German attack on 21 July 1944 was not the first incursion of German or Vichy French forces into the Vercors fortress. On 22 January and 18 March 1944 smaller German detachments investigated the plateau, but left the Maquis and the local population relatively unharmed. On 29 January Reserve Pionier Bataillon 7 destroyed the Maquis de Malleval on the northern fringes of the Vercors. Three months later, between 16 and 23 April 1944, the French Milice staged a larger operation on the plateau, but concluded in their after-action report that the number of Maquisards had been 'considerably exaggerated when compared to reality'. Two Maquisards were killed, four wounded and nine taken prisoner. In addition the Milice burnt a few houses. The Germans did not seem to be too happy with the results of this operation. Hence, 157. Reserve Division planned its own major operation for May (Operation *Bergen*), but it was cancelled for

Members of the French Milice take two Maquisards into custody during an inconclusive operation in the Vercors in spring 1944. As a result the German Sipo/SD no longer used the Milice for future military operations. (Mémorial de Caen)

unknown reasons. Overall, both the occupiers and Vichy considered the Maquis du Vercors a potential but not an imminent threat prior to D-Day.

This all changed during the night of 8–9 June 1944. The Maquis du Vercors was thought to have received the code message for mobilization from BBC London: 'Le chamois des Alpes bondit' (the chamois of the Alps jumps up). The German reaction was not long in coming. On 13 June a company of Reserve Grenadier Bataillon 179, supported by elements of Reserve Artillerie Abteilung 7 (deployed in an infantry role), attacked the Maquis' positions around the village of St Nizier, the gateway to the Vercors plateau. Three Maquis companies defended the sector with unexpected determination. One of the company commanders was Jean Prévost ('Goderville'), a respected novelist in France by that time. Although without any proper training as a military commander, he displayed genuine tactical skills as a leader. Finally, after several hours of fighting the Germans were compelled to withdraw to Grenoble and lost one man killed and eight wounded; French losses totalled eight killed and four wounded. This engagement at St Nizier on 13 June signalled a new departure in anti-partisan operations in France; for the first time the Germans were unable to defeat a partisan force in an open, albeit small, battle. There has been some debate about how serious this German attempt was. Did the Germans really think they were able to storm the plateau with these relatively weak forces? Or was it just a probing attack? In all likelihood the latter seems to have been the case.

Two days later on 15 June the Germans staged a second attempt to take hold of St Nizier. This time the contingent was reinforced by further elements of Reserve Pionier Bataillon 7 and Reserve Grenadier Regiment 157, and some Milice units, in total probably around 1,000 men. After a few hours the battle was over; the Maquis was forced to withdraw with the loss of 24 men killed. The Germans had six men killed and fifteen wounded. In addition, they set St Nizier on fire as reprisal. With the destroyed village in German hands the door to the Vercors fortress seemed to be open, but the Germans did not immediately exploit their success. In the following days Huet renounced any attempt to retake St Nizier and instead considered the new shorter defensive line around Lans an advantage.

The fighting for St Nizier stood as a warning for both sides; on the one hand the Germans were now aware that destroying the Maquis du Vercors would be a costly operation and required more than just a few locally available units. A carefully planned operation was required instead. The Resistance on the other hand had to realize that mobilization had come too early and they had not been able to ward off a larger German onslaught. The Vercors could only be held if, first, the Allied forces landed soon in southern France and, second, the Vercors was to be reinforced. In the following days and weeks the leaders of the Vercors sent numerous telegrams to London and Algiers, all requesting weapons and even regular airborne forces. However, initially the support was almost negligible. Only two minor drops occurred on 13–14 June near La Chapelle, followed by another on 25 June. Owing to the short hours of darkness in summer, the RAF had only a very small time slot available for aircraft starting in the UK to carry out night drops into Southern France.

This changed when the USAAF decided in July to fly day drops. The Maquis had designated seven different drop zones on the plateau. The two largest were permanently manned, with one situated near Vassieux ('Taille-Crayon') for planes coming from Algiers and the other near La Chapelle ('Rayon') for flights from the United Kingdom. Eventually, on 14 July, the French national day, the Maquis du Vercors was able to regain hope when 72 B-17s dropped 860 containers with weapons and other supplies. Most of the men on the plateau could now be armed with automatic weapons, mainly Stens, Brens and Thompsons. Additionally they also received a number of anti-tank bazookas. But any elation was considerably marred when the French came to realize that the Allies had again not supplied them with the heavy weapons so desperately needed to defend the plateau, particularly its north-eastern parts. At least the 15 men of OG 'Justine' and the seven men of Inter-Allied Mission 'Eucalyptus' had parachuted onto the plateau by late June. Although none of these men had any information about an expected imminent landing in southern France, the leaders of the Vercors felt their arrival meant that Algiers had not forgotten the Resistance fighters on the plateau. Moreover, Eucalyptus's operational orders had probably been misread, misinterpreted or just ignored. True, Longe's and Houseman's instructions stated that mortars could be expected later that month when technical problems with the detonators would have been rectified for air drops. However, 'Eucalyptus' also had to point out to the commanders on the plateau: 'True guerrilla tactics do not require the employment of heavy weapons and that present policy is to supply these weapons on an ad hoc basis only.' In addition, the SOE advised only small operations at the moment. The FFI commanders on the plateau could suggest plans for operations on a larger scale and forward them via 'Eucalyptus', but for support they would need SOE's approval first. This was the root of the tragedy of the Maquis du Vercors that unfolded in the coming weeks.

Meanwhile the Germans reorganized their forces. After having intercepted a message from London to the French Resistance ordering it to keep its action to the absolute minimum, Generalleutnant Pflaum sought to take advantage of the situation and tried to regain the initiative by mounting a series of offensive operations against the local Maquis. Between 3 and 6 July the Germans defeated the Maquis in the Massif des Bauges east of Chambéry. A few days later the majority of the mountain infantry battalions transferred to the southern Jura. In conjunction with various Eastern troops they disrupted the local Maquis in the large-scale Operation *Treffenfeld* (10–19 July), but could not defeat them conclusively. For a third time after the operations earlier in February and April the Maquis in the Jura dispersed in time, only to reappear once the Germans had left the area.

On 8 July, even before the start of *Treffenfeld*, Generalleutnant Niehoff had ordered preparation for a general attack against the Maquis du Vercors under the codename *Bettina*. Evidently, the container drops in the Vercors on 14 July enhanced the German concerns about the threat to the rear of their forces on the Mediterranean coast. The *Gebirgsjäger* of 157. Reserve Division were prematurely withdrawn from *Treffenfeld* and sent on a forced march to the Vercors. On 20 July the build-up was completed, the plateau encircled by German forces. Niehoff was in charge of the entire operation; Pflaum remained in control of the units from his 157. Reserve Division which played a crucial role in the oncoming operation.

At the same time the Luftwaffe had increased its presence in the skies over the Vercors. Just after the American B-17s had finished their drops on 14 July fighter-bombers of the Kampfgeschwader Bongart appeared and machine-gunned Maquisards who were recovering the containers. In the afternoon and on the following day a number of Ju 88s and Re 2002s bombed the provisional airstrips on the plateau as well as the villages of La Chapelle and Vassieux; both as a result were badly hit. In Vassieux only four out of 85 buildings remained intact; almost half of the buildings were deemed totally destroyed. The Luftwaffe could operate as it pleased without Allied interdiction; all messages from the Vercors to Algiers and London, urging the Allies to bomb German airfields, particularly Chabeuil near Valence, remained unanswered. In the following days the unimpeded presence of German planes over the battlefield would turn out to be a major factor in their victory.

THE GENERAL GERMAN ATTACK AND BREAK-IN

The airborne landing at Vassieux

It was to become a sunny and hot summer day on 21 July. From early morning the French civilian labour company was out in the fields near Vassieux and continued its work on the provisional airstrip codenamed Taille-Crayon (Vassieux); after many days of hard work the project was finally just about finished. Suddenly, at around 0900hrs the skies were filled with planes. The workers and Maquisards greeted them with joy; as they were coming from the south they believed them to be Allied aircraft bringing supply drops. However, a few moments later the Frenchmen's faces turned pale; instead of the USAAF white star or the RAF blue–white–red roundel, the planes bore the German Iron Cross on their wings. Now events moved fast; at 60 degrees the gliders nosedived towards the ground before they opened a braking parachute at about 300m altitude. Silently the gliders floated down. It was the calm before the storm. Shortly afterwards they touched ground, and German paratroopers stormed out of the hulls. The German attack against the Vercors citadel had just started with an unexpected airborne landing right in the heart of the plateau.

The Germans had already used gliders with stunning success on several occasions in the war: at Eben-Emael in May 1940, on Crete in May 1941 and at the Gran Sasso in September 1943 to rescue Mussolini. One veteran of Eben-Emael and Crete was Friedrich Schäfer, then still an NCO. Born in 1919 in the working-class district of Gelsenkirchen-Buer in the Ruhr, he had been promoted through the ranks and finally commissioned in 1942 owing to the bravery he had displayed on all major German airborne operations during the war. Schäfer was a keen and ambitious officer, but also a fervent supporter of National-Socialist ideology. As an *Oberleutnant* he was appointed commander of the airborne element of the operation in the Vercors. Since 8 June 1944 Schäfer had commanded 7. Kompanie/ Kampfgeschwader (KG) 200 and prepared his men for this special operation. His superior, Oberst Heinrich Heigl, ensured that 7./KG 200 would be deployed as a single strike force and not piecemeal as in various other operations elsewhere against the French Maquis. Yet the Vercors would become the single most significant ground operation KG 200 carried out in its entire existence.

In strict secrecy a number of DFS 230 gliders from I./ LLG 1 had been moved by road from Nancy to Lyon-Bron, and later to Chabeuil airfield near Valence on 14 July. The DFS 230 was the standard German glider in World War II. It was normally towed by an He 111 or Do 17 and could transport one section. Once landed the pilot provided fire support with his MG15 mounted on each glider. For the Vercors operation the Germans fitted the gliders with additional retro-rockets to shorten their landing run.

German glider pilots from I./LLG 1 at Chabeuil airfield in the early hours of the morning on 21 July 1944, moments before the start of the operation. In the background is one of the He 111s used as towing aircraft for the DFS 230. (Stijn David)

AIRBORNE LANDING AT VASSIEUX, 21 JULY 1944 (pp. 40–41)

In the first years of World War II the Wehrmacht had conducted several major airborne operations, most prominently in Rotterdam, at Eben Emael and on Crete. However, in the second half of the war these operations were limited to commando-style raids involving not more than a handful of companies, for example, at the Gran Sasso or at Drvar. Another operation was the airborne landing of 7. Kompanie/Kampfgeschwader 200 (KG 200), in the heart of the Vercors plateau at Vassieux-en-Vercors against the French Resistance. During the previous days Geschwader Bongart had bombarded and destroyed parts of Vassieux **(1)**. In the summer of 1944 this wing was exclusively deployed in anti-partisan operations in France and also provided close air support for the glider landing at Vassieux with Re 2002s, Italian fighter-bombers **(2)**. At around 0930hrs the first wave with seven DFS 230 gliders from Luftlandegeschwader 1 landed next to the hamlets of Les Jossauds, La Mure and Le Château, about a kilometre north of the village. The artwork depicts the second wave, which touched ground on the fringes of Vassieux at 1000hrs under Oberleutnant Friedrich Schäfer, the overall commander of this airborne operation. Between 12 and 15 DFS 230 gliders land with this wave **(3)**. Smoke grenades are dropped **(4)**, the

nine-man crews jump out of the hull of each glider and the pilots provide fire support with their MG15s **(5)**. The German *Fallschirmjäger* storm into the village where, after overcoming the initial shock, the French Maquisards of 11e Régiment de Cuirassiers offer stubborn resistance from the houses **(6)**. But the Germans prevail and mop up Vassieux within an hour. Soon after, however, they find themselves exposed to fierce French counter-attacks; besieged in the village over the following days the *Fallschirmjäger* are eventually relieved on 25 July 1944 by friendly forces coming from the south of the plateau. With the airborne forces, members of the Sicherheitspolizei und Sicherheitsdienst (Security Police and Security Service) from Lyon take part in this operation, probably accompanied by some French collaborators. Amongst the police forces is their commander, SS-Obersturmbannführer Dr Werner Knab, who was previously involved in mass crimes in the Ukraine **(7)**. Some sources suggest that Knab had a reputation for being a rather weak and cowardly person and for wanting to take part in this risky airborne operation only to prove he and his security policemen could act like soldiers. Knab certainly directed some of the atrocities the Germans committed against civilians right after the landing **(8)**.

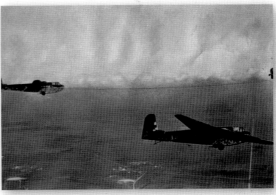

In the morning of 21 July the airborne force took off from Chabeuil airfield; when reaching the southern edge of the Vercors, the transport planes released the gliders, still around 8km from their designated target. Although the Maquis du Drôme signalled the arrival of an airborne force to their colleagues on the plateau, it was far too late to put together an effective defence force. The surprise was complete, the gliders landed with breathtaking precision: two in close proximity to the hamlet of La Mure, two at Le Chateau and three at Les Jossauds. The German *Fallschirmjäger* threw grenades through the windows of the buildings and stormed the houses. Indiscriminately, they shot at everything that moved, be it Maquisards, civilians or cattle. A group of around 30 Maquisards was caught asleep in La Mure; the Germans killed them all before they could realize what was happening. At the same time aircraft from Kampfgeschwader Bongart provided close air support by machine-gunning the workers on the Taille-Crayon airstrip and bombarding the village and Maquis positions.

Thanks to the element of surprise the first landing wave fully achieved its objectives; after only a few minutes all northern access roads to Vassieux, including the important intersections, were firmly in the hands of the *Fallschirmjäger*. The Germans had destroyed all the enemy camps that their intelligence had identified prior to the operation in this confined area. The *Fallschirmjäger* now prepared for defence in the farmhouses at La Mure, Le Chateau and Les Jossauds. Any French reinforcements from La Chapelle or St Agnan would have to cross large killing areas covered by MG42s and light mortars. The *Fallschirmjäger*'s shock and terror tactics had horrible consequences not only for the Maquis, but also for the civilian population. Around 20 civilians were killed by the first landing wave.

Yet only around 80 German soldiers had landed so far. In late morning the second wave approached the plains around Vassieux; it carried the majority of 7./KG 200, amongst them Schäfer and SS-Obersturmbannführer Werner Knab. By taking part in this dangerous mission Knab obviously wanted to prove to the Wehrmacht that he and his Sipo/SD men could operate in exactly the same way as the military. Moreover, he would be able to control the reprisals in whatever way he deemed appropriate for the 'terrorists' at Vassieux. Knab was probably accompanied by a few French collaborators. It remains unclear whether *Osttruppen* also fought around Vassieux on 21 July. However, it is certain that no SS troops landed, as has often been wrongly claimed.

In contrast to the first wave, the second wave with Schäfer and his 150 men landed much closer to the village, but the element of surprise was now lost. The Maquis saluted the gliders with heavy machine-gun fire; two gliders

Towed DFS 230s minutes before release. To achieve maximum surprise the Germans flew in from the south of the plateau, i.e. where the FFI expected Allied reinforcement to come in from Algiers. (Stija David and MRV)

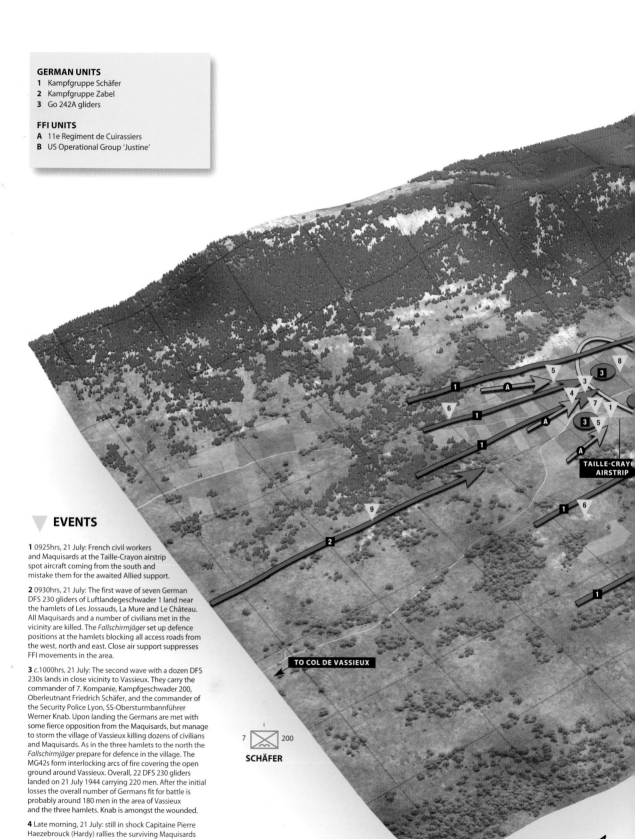

GERMAN UNITS
1 Kampfgruppe Schäfer
2 Kampfgruppe Zabel
3 Go 242A gliders

FFI UNITS
A 11e Regiment de Cuirassiers
B US Operational Group 'Justine'

TAILLE-CRAY
AIRSTRIP

TO COL DE VASSIEUX

7 ⊠ 200
SCHÄFER

▼ EVENTS

1 0925hrs, 21 July: French civil workers
and Maquisards at the Taille-Crayon airstrip
spot aircraft coming from the south and
mistake them for the awaited Allied support.

2 0930hrs, 21 July: The first wave of seven German
DFS 230 gliders of Luftlandegeschwader 1 land near
the hamlets of Les Jossauds, La Mure and Le Château.
All Maquisards and a number of civilians met in the
vicinity are killed. The *Fallschirmjäger* set up defence
positions at the hamlets blocking all access roads from
the west, north and east. Close air support suppresses
FFI movements in the area.

3 *c.*1000hrs, 21 July: The second wave with a dozen DFS
230s lands in close vicinity to Vassieux. They carry the
commander of 7. Kompanie, Kampfgeschwader 200,
Oberleutnant Friedrich Schäfer, and the commander of
the Security Police Lyon, SS-Obersturmbannführer
Werner Knab. Upon landing the Germans are met with
some fierce opposition from the Maquisards, but manage
to storm the village of Vassieux killing dozens of civilians
and Maquisards. As in the three hamlets to the north the
Fallschirmjäger prepare for defence in the village. The
MG42s form interlocking arcs of fire covering the open
ground around Vassieux. Overall, 22 DFS 230 gliders
landed on 21 July 1944 carrying 220 men. After the initial
losses the overall number of Germans fit for battle is
probably around 180 men in the area of Vassieux
and the three hamlets. Knab is amongst the wounded.

4 Late morning, 21 July: still in shock Capitaine Pierre
Haezebrouck (Hardy) rallies the surviving Maquisards
and civil workers from the airstrip and launches a hasty
counter-attack from the south-east. The attack fails in
the hail of MG42 fire as the French cross the open
ground. Haezebrouck falls in this battle.

Note: Gridlines are shown at intervals of 500mtrs/546yds

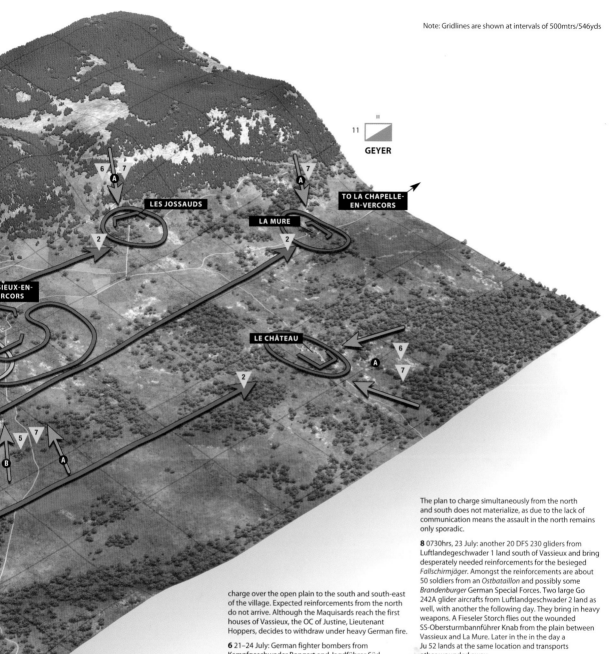

III
11   GEYER

LES JOSSAUDS

LA MURE

TO LA CHAPELLE-EN-VERCORS

...IEUX-EN-...RCORS

LE CHÂTEAU

...O COL DE SAINT-...IS/COL DE ROUSSET

charge over the open plain to the south and south-east of the village. Expected reinforcements from the north do not arrive. Although the Maquisards reach the first houses of Vassieux, the OC of Justine, Lieutenant Hoppers, decides to withdraw under heavy German fire.

6 21–24 July: German fighter bombers from Kampfgeschwader Bongart and Jagdführer Süd relentlessly strafe and bomb Maquis positions around Vassieux, even on 22 July, a largely overcast day.

7 0200hrs, 23 July: postponed a several times and for more than 12 hours overall, the third French attempt to re-take Vassieux commences under the command of Capitaine Maurice Bourgeois (Bataille). Although outnumbering the Germans by about four to one and supported by a Hotchkiss 25mm anti-aircraft gun, the attack utterly fails. Ill-coordinated fire and manoeuvre as well as the illumination of the battlefield by the Germans contribute to high losses amongst the Maquisards.

The plan to charge simultaneously from the north and south does not materialize, as due to the lack of communication means the assault in the north remains only sporadic.

8 0730hrs, 23 July: another 20 DFS 230 gliders from Luftlandegeschwader 1 land south of Vassieux and bring desperately needed reinforcements for the besieged *Fallschirmjäger*. Amongst the reinforcements are about 50 soldiers from an *Ostbataillon* and possibly some *Brandenburger* German Special Forces. Two large Go 242A glider aircrafts from Luftlandegeschwader 2 land as well, with another the following day. They bring in heavy weapons. A Fieseler Storch flies out the wounded SS-Obersturmbannführer Knab from the plain between Vassieux and La Mure. Later in the in the day a Ju 52 lands at the same location and transports other wounded away.

Exhausted and tired the French abandon the plan for a fourth attack. Although the general dispersal order is given for all FFI forces in the Vercors during the afternoon of 23 July, a sporadic encirclement ring is still kept around Vassieux.

9 Morning, 25 July: *Panzergrenadiere* of Kampfgruppe Zabel relieve the *Fallschirmjäger* of 7./KG 200. The Germans withdraw from the ruins of Vassieux northwards to La Chapelle. Kampfgruppe Zabel returns to the Drôme Valley on 25 or 26 July.

5 Afternoon, 21 July: Huet orders Capitaine Narcisse Geyer (Thivollet), the commander of the 11e Regiment de Cuirassiers and the FFI forces in the southern sector of the Vercors, to organise a prepared attack on Vassieux. Around 400 men supported by Brens and mortars charge the provisionally entrenched *Fallschirmjäger*. The 15 men of the US Operational Group 'Justine' take part in the attack. Again the French forces

THE AIRBORNE LANDING AND FIGHTING AT VASSIEUX-EN-VERCORS, 21–25 JULY 1944

German gliders land in a commando-style operation in the heart of the Vercors plateau crashed, one of them carrying the company's medic. Yet the Germans were able to penetrate the ruined village and expelled the remaining Maquisards, albeit with increasing losses. Knab was amongst the first casualties and was wounded in the leg. In the ruined village the Germans 'hedgehogged' in and formed intersecting arcs of fire west, south and eastwards with their MG42s. Instead of pushing towards La Chapelle and St Agnan as had been initially planned, around 200 survivors of KG 200 now found themselves on the defensive. Their situation deteriorated further within the next few hours; fate seemed to be starting to favour the French.

After having overcome the initial shock the young Capitaine Pierre Haezebrouck ('Hardy') rallied all available Maquisards around Vassieux. He had been guarding the Taille-Crayon airstrip with his men and was now in command of the first hasty counter-attack against the German-occupied village. Fighting fiercely, the French got as far as the outskirts before heavy German machine-gun fire and close air support forced them to withdraw. The Maquis's lack of heavy support weapons became painfully apparent. Haezebrouck fell in this engagement.

Already during late morning, the FFI had sent an initial message from the plateau to Algiers: 'Are being attacked by parachutists. We defend.' This telegram, however, remained unanswered. Shortly after, Major Longe transmitted another message to SOE in Algiers. He demanded the deployment of Free French airborne forces on the plateau and the bombardment of Chabeuil airfield to disrupt the German air support. Longe also pointed out the danger of terrible German reprisals should the Maquis lose this battle. But for the time being, Longe also received no answer.

Yet time seemed to be on the side of the French; in the evening a thunderstorm moved over the plateau, after which the weather remained cloudy. As a consequence, Kampfgruppe Schäfer could not expect any reinforcements, nor supplies, or any close air support. Therefore, Huet decided to launch a second counter-attack; retaking Vassieux was now his top priority. He therefore ordered all available reserves, mainly the

An aerial photograph showing the plains around Vassieux from south to north. The photo was taken by a German reconnaissance aircraft in preparation for the operation in July 1944. The majority of the gliders landed to the south and east of Vassieux. (IWM)

11e Cuirassiers, to Vassieux and entrusted Capitaine Geyer with the execution of the mission. In late afternoon 400 Frenchmen assaulted around 150 German defenders provisionally entrenched in the ruins of Vassieux. The attackers even had three mortars, two Bren machine guns and some bazookas available to them. The 15 Americans of Operational Group 'Justine' supported the attack as well. Again the FFI was able to reach the first houses in the south-eastern corner of Vassieux, but the commander of 'Justine', Captain Hopper, decided to withdraw – prematurely as some critics would later claim with the benefit of hindsight. The main problem, however, was the direction of the attack; the French had stormed over the largely open ground to the south of the village. In addition, they had expected reinforcements from the north; but these forces had never shown up for reasons unknown. A few hours later Geyer reported the failed attack to Descour and Huet; he also had to convey the sad news that the Descour's son Jacques had fallen in the battle.

Capitaine Narcisse Geyer (1912–1993), the commander of 11e Régiment de Cuirassiers and the forces of the southern sector in the Vercors. Between 21 and 23 July 1944 his unit launched several counter-attacks against the German airborne force at Vassieux, all to no avail. (MRV)

On the following morning of 22 July the skies partly cleared again. The Luftwaffe dropped some supply containers for their besieged men at Vassieux. Kampfgruppe Schäfer used the time available to reinforce its defensive positions in the ruins of the village and the surrounding hamlets. Indeed, Huet and Geyer insisted on another attempt to retake Vassieux and now entrusted Capitaine Maurice Bourgeois ('Bataille') with the execution of this vital and pressing mission. As commander of the 1er Escadron/11e Cuirassiers, Bourgeois fixed the time for the attack at 1245hrs. Impatiently his men waited in the forest south of Vassieux when suddenly the Luftwaffe started bombing their positions and strafed the open ground around the village. In the inferno Bourgeois lost contact with some of his subordinate units and decided to attack later in the day hoping the Luftwaffe's impact would lessen at dusk. Indeed, the Luftwaffe had dropped 15 tons of bombs around Vassieux during these two days.

Postponed once again, Bourgeois's forces finally assaulted at 0200hrs on 23 July. The *Fallschirmjäger* quickly fired illuminating grenades behind the French forces crossing the open ground. The attackers' silhouettes hence became easy prey for the German MGs and mortars. The war diary of the 11e Cuirassiers noted the assault failed owing to 'lack of coordination in manoeuvre'. As a former, albeit very young, regular officer Bourgeois should have realized the impossibility of carrying out a night attack with inexperienced troops, as the vast majority of his men were. Another counter-attack – the fourth overall – was planned for 23 July, but eventually cancelled. The Maquisards were tired and demoralized. Huet chose to relieve a good number of the besieging forces and sent fresh units of the 14e BCA from the Forêt de Lente to the Vassieux front. In this remote part of the plateau these men had not yet learnt about the dramatic military situation.

On the morning of 23 July the situation at Vassieux reached stalemate. The French had been unable to destroy the German airborne force despite all the reinforcements they had brought into the battle. German-occupied Vassieux was like a poisoned thorn in the defenders' flesh. However, Kampfgruppe Schäfer, too, had been unable to execute its plans. It suffered very heavy losses on the first day alone: 22 men killed and 29 wounded, which totalled around a quarter of its original strength. Instead of being on the offensive, the *Fallschirmjäger* were besieged in Vassieux and the surrounding hamlets; they had to fight in isolation because of the poor weather, and support and supply from the air remained limited. Kampfgruppe Schäfer needed to be relieved as soon as possible by ground forces. Thus, everything depended on the speed of the advance of the other three *Kampfgruppen*: Zabel, Schwehr and Seeger.

The swift advance of Kampfgruppe Zabel in the south

Major Zabel's *Panzergrenadiere* were the best armed of all four attacking German *Kampfgruppen* and even had armoured transport vehicles available. Zabel's armoured infantry from 9. Panzer Division was supported by elements of Marschbataillon Müller from 352. Infanterie Division and probably also by an *Ostbataillon* company whose identity still remains unclear today. Kampfgruppe Zabel's mission was to seal off the Vercors from the south. The operations had already started prior to the general German attack with the clearing of the access routes to the Drôme river valley. On 19 July the Germans took Vaunaveys and a day later, without battle, the provincial town of Crest; soldiers from an eastern unit followed the *Panzergrenadiere* and sacked the town. This was a precursor of things to come on the plateau. On 21 July Kampfgruppe Zabel left the open terrain and started its onslaught into the Drôme mountain valley along Departmental Road No. 93. The local FFI commander, 48-year-old Paul Pons, hoped to delay the German advance with a series of ambushes at specific geographic points. Only a few kilometres into the Drôme Valley the German column was ambushed for the first time. According to French sources the Germans lost five lorries and suffered heavy casualties. However, the *Panzergrenadiere*'s casualty lists did not mention a single loss. The German column quickly continued its advance; in the early afternoon the FFI laid further ambushes around the Saillans railway tunnel and the Espenel bridge. This time the French offered a more sustained resistance. All afternoon skirmishes raged in the vicinity of the small town but in the end, the Germans prevailed with close air support provided by elements of Kampfgeschwader Bongart. The losses of the *Panzergrenadiere* totalled three men killed and six wounded whilst those of Marschbataillon Müller are unknown; French losses were 14 men killed and a number of wounded. Six civilians also died in this engagement or were shot by the Germans in reprisal. Furthermore, Espenel was partly burned down.

A modern photo showing the attack sector of Reserve Gebirgsjäger Bataillon II/98 on 21 July 1944. The Pas de Bachassons (red circle) was 7. Kompanie's objective, the Pas de la Selle that of 8. Kompanie. (Author's collection)

The fighting in the south of the Vercors Plateau, 19–29 July 1944

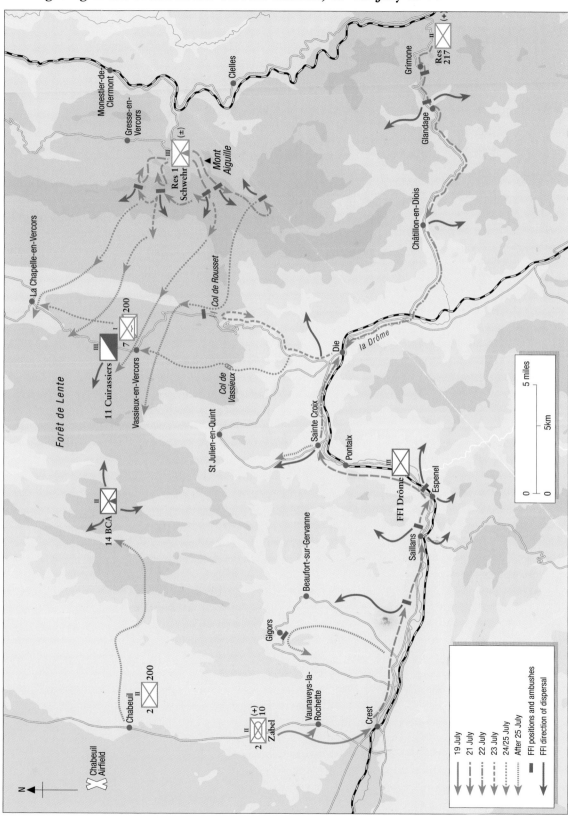

Res 217 (+)

Grimone

Glandage

Monestier-de-Clermont

Cielles

Gresse-en-Vercors

Res 1 Schwehr (±)

Mont Aiguille

Châtillon-en-Diois

La Chapelle-en-Vercors

7 200

11 Cuirassiers

Vassieux-en-Vercors

Col de Rousset

Die

la Drôme

Col de Vassieux

Forêt de Lente

St Julien-en-Quint

Sainte Croix

Pontaix

FFI Drôme

Espenel

14 BCA

Saillans

Beaufort-sur-Gervanne

Gigors

2 200

Chabeuil

Vaunaveys-la-Rochette

Crest

2 10 Zabel (+)

Chabeuil Airfield

N

5 miles

5km

0

0

19 July
21 July
22 July
23 July
24/25 July
After 25 July
FFI positions and ambushes
FFI direction of dispersal

49

Nevertheless, the road to Die was not yet open to the Germans. Pons ordered his subordinate Pierre Raynaud ('Alain') to hold Pontaix and Sainte-Croix with his men; communist FTPFs supported the defence. Overall, 600 Frenchmen were supposed to ward off Kampfgruppe Zabel's march through the valley whatever the costs might be. However, when the Germans reached the bridge over the Drôme near Pontaix, they found the French positions abandoned. Raynaud had renounced any opposition and declared himself to have obeyed SOE orders instead which had stated that any contact with larger German contingents was to be avoided. Raynaud's decision sparked a huge controversy amongst the FFI. He was soon blamed for having been unable to mould his Maquis group into a fighting force, but had rather kept them as a loose and ill-disciplined bunch of scoundrels. He was replaced after the Pontaix–Sainte-Croix affair and, on 8 August, arrested. It took SOE Major Cammaert's personal intervention to free his own protégé.

Having missed the final opportunity to stop the German column, the FFI hastily evacuated Die; the remaining fighters moved northwards to the Vercors plateau. Those Maquisards who had been wounded in the engagements in the Drôme Valley had to stay in the hospital and were left to the mercy of the Germans. When Kampfgruppe Zabel entered the town on 22 July it showed no pity and executed them. Meanwhile, a smaller *Kampfgruppe* consisting mainly of Reserve Grenadier Bataillon 217 and a few minor detachments had come from the east over the Col de Grimone after some sporadic fighting and linked with Kampfgruppe Zabel east of Die. The encirclement of the Vercors plateau was now complete.

Kampfgruppe Zabel had thus fulfilled its mission and reached its objectives faster than originally expected. This offered the Germans a tempting option: to launch an attack onto the plateau from the south. For the French, the battles to the south of the plateau were not only a disaster on a tactical level but, furthermore, meant the loss of any contact with FFI forces farther south. The Maquis du Vercors was now fully cut off and isolated, an organized retreat to the south impossible.

A German aerial reconnaissance photo depicting the east face of the Vercors plateau where the *Gebirgsjäger* of Kampfgruppe Schwehr attacked. In the left background is the highest mountain of the massif, le Grand Veymont. (IWM)

Kampfgruppe Schwehr and the fight for the mountain passes in the south-east

The Vercors's reputation as a natural fortress was mainly due to the steep mountain walls on its eastern face which stretch about 60km from north-west of Grenoble to the south. Whilst these walls seem to be almost insurmountable, the mountains fall away very gently on the western side. Only about a dozen small mountain passes allow a crossing from east to west. All these passes are very narrow, a few of them, such as the Pas de la Ville, only a few metres wide. Hence the passes can be reached only by steep footpaths; roads or bridle paths did not and still do not exist. Only a few tiny roads wind along the slopes at the bottom of the walls, passing through a handful of modest mountain villages. The plains to the west of the ridge are uninhabited and covered with extensive forests, only occasionally broken by Alpine pastures with shepherds' huts for the summer season.

These remote parts of the Vercors did not play a major role in French defence planning. Huet and his staff considered this terrain unsuitable for heavy weapons and therefore believed the Germans would be unable to exploit their main advantage in this area: their firepower. Furthermore, the passes in the south-east were far from any infrastructure and the key villages of the plateau. As a consequence the French deployed only a single company in this sector, the Compagnie André with about 150 men. Each pass was guarded by around 10 to 20 Maquisards armed with rifles, light machine guns and a few light mortars.

Generalleutnant Pflaum was well aware of this weakness in the enemy's order of battle and decided to do the unexpected; one battle group would attack over the passes. For the *Gebirgsjäger* in his division this was exactly the kind of terrain they were trained to fight in. In various operations against the Maquis they had shown their physical robustness and military skills. Their heavy weapons could be easily loaded on mules and with practice the mountain guns could be assembled ready to fire in about ten minutes. The light 2cm mortars were even more flexible and the ideal mountain infantry support weapons against 'soft' targets.

Oberst Schwehr had been in charge during almost all previous operations against the Maquis in difficult mountain terrain; he seemed to be the right commander to take the passes in the south-east. For his mission he had the Reserve Gebirgsjäger Bataillone I/98 and II/98 available as well as one and a half companies of Reserve Gebirgs Artillerie Abteilung 79. Overall the Germans could deploy around 1,200 to 1,500 men in Kampfgruppe Schwehr. The odds were therefore between 8:1 and 10:1 against the Maquis; the heavy weapons benefited the Germans, too, and at least in theory they could also count on support from the air. However, the French could defend in terrain which immensely favoured the defender. Unfortunately, they seemingly did not make any effort to fortify their positions in the passes. This negligence turned out to be fatal.

Schwehr decided not to attack all the passes, but picked just four of them instead and split his forces accordingly into two groups. Reserve Gebirgsjäger Bataillon I/98 was to take the extremely narrow Pas de la Ville and the Pas de Berrièves with the support of one mountain artillery company. Farther to the south Reserve Gebirgsjäger Bataillon II/98 was to take possession of the Pas de Chattons and the Pas de la Selle. Hauptmann Clemens Graf Rességuier de Miremont, a very capable battalion commander, charged his 7. Kompanie with taking the Pas de Bachassons and later the Pas de Chattons and his

FIGHTING AT THE PAS DE LA SELLE, 21 JULY 1944 (pp. 52–53)

As a consequence of their experience in the Alps during World War I the German army formed *Gebirgsjäger* units which specialized in mountain warfare. Overall ten mountain divisions were raised during World War II, but they were mostly used as ordinary infantry and saw action in mountainous areas only on a few occasions, most notably in the Caucasus in 1942–43. Another example was the combat against the French Resistance in the Alps in 1944, where Reserve Gebirgsjäger Regiment 1 of 157. Reserve Division was deployed. The division and regiment were normally training formations for young recruits with battle-experienced cadres. For the Vercors operation the *Gebirgsjäger* were tasked with seizing four steep mountain passes in the south-east of the Vercors massif. The artwork shows the fighting at the most southern of these passes, the Pas de la Selle, on 21 July 1944. In the late afternoon Gebirgsjäger of 8. Kompanie/Reserve Gebirgsjäger Bataillon II/98, together with four attached machine-gun sections from 9. Kompanie as well as a heavy mortar and an infantry support gun section from 10. Kompanie climbed the pass. The battalion headquarters under Hauptmann Graf Clemens Rességuier de Miremont also followed 8. Kompanie. When the force had almost reached the Pas de la Selle the French Maquis of Compagnie André started to fire from above **(1)** and a fierce battle ensued. The two most forward German platoons, platoon Wilhelm **(2)** and platoon Hilche **(3)**, have stalled and cannot move any farther. For the time being the third platoon under the command of Oberleutnant Hans Schlemmer cannot join the battle **(4)**. In this critical situation the officer commanding 8. Kompanie, Leutnant Stefan Ritter, orders the deployment of the attached heavy weapons. But it takes almost an hour for these to be brought forward. When they open fire a hail of mortar and machine-gun fire rains down on the French defenders **(5)**. Effectively directed by non-commissioned officers **(6)**, the heavy machine guns from 9. Kompanie turn out to be a crucial factor. The amount of firepower and the following swift advance of the left forward platoon **(2)** finally tips the battle in favour of the Germans. At 2115hrs the *Gebirgsjäger* finally seize the pass from the heavily outnumbered French defenders. Since Reserve Gebirgsjäger Regiment 1 was only a training formation, it was not issued with the most recent equipment. Instead of the modern MG42 the young recruits had to rely on the older MG34 **(7)**. Despite the Wehrmacht's advanced communication technology in their armoured forces, their infantry units normally had only radios from battalion and sometimes company level upwards. Communication on the lower tactical levels had to be done by runners **(8)**.

8. Kompanie with the Pas de la Selle. Each company had a heavy machine-gun section and a medium mortar section attached from 9. and 10. Kompanie. The 8. Kompanie was to bear the brunt of the battalion's main effort and had in addition at its disposal a heavy machine-gun platoon, an infantry gun platoon and a section of engineers. Rességuier's battalion headquarters moved with 8. Kompanie and he also had radio contact with the division. Overall this force counted about 600 men.

In the morning and early afternoon of 21 July Kampfgruppe Schwehr investigated the hamlets and the forests on the bottom of the steep slopes to the plateau. This search was time-consuming, but absolutely necessary. Once on the plateau the battle group's supply routes would hang by a thread. Any undetected smaller enemy groups in the valleys could later block the narrow, but vital footpaths leading up to the passes and therefore endanger all of Kampfgruppe Schwehr's supply. However, the German search for any Maquisards in the approaches to the plateau remained inconclusive, no enemy forces were met. In the late afternoon the *Gebirgsjäger* climbed the slopes leading up to the plateau and deployed for battle about 300m below the passes. The entire battle at the Pas de la Selle lasted little more than an hour. Then the Maquisards routed; at 1900hrs the pass was in the hands of 8. Kompanie. Their casualties remained remarkably low with one killed and six wounded who were transported back to the valley. It seems the company had requisitioned some French civilians as bearers. The Germans formed in a 'hedgehog' position and bivouacked at the Pas de la Selle in the pouring rain.

Around the same time on the evening of 21 July the neighbouring Pas de Bachassons and Pas de Chattons, also came under German control. Here 7. Kompanie/Reserve Gebirgsjäger Bataillon II/98 had successfully attacked and suffered slightly higher casualties than its colleagues at the Pas de la Selle: One German soldier was killed, 11 wounded. The *Gebirgsjäger*'s superior leadership, training and experience, together with the heavy weapons and the element of surprise, left the outnumbered Maquisards with no chance. The high ratio between killed and wounded on the German side also demonstrated the poor standard of French marksmanship. Nevertheless, the FFI were at least able to hold the Pas de la Ville and the Pas de Berrièves on 21 July. Despite a relatively massive artillery support, Reserve Gebirgsjäger Bataillon I/98 could not get a foothold on these two passes. However, as the battalion's casualty lists for that day display only three men killed and another three wounded (amongst them one lieutenant), it is probable that the Germans did not try to conquer both passes at any cost.

Despite its firm stand at the Pas de la Ville and the Pas de Berrièves the French Compagnie André had fought a futile battle from the start. The men went into battle with immense confidence and optimism, relying on the terrain which favoured the defenders to such a great extent. However, their morale was soon to shrink. After early news of the German airborne operation at Vassieux reached the defenders at the passes, there was concern that *Fallschirmjäger* might also attempt a landing to the rear of Compagnie André at Grande Cabane. Thus the sector commander, Geyer, ordered another company to reinforce the passes. However this turned out to be more challenging than expected. Communication between headquarters and the troops at the passes was difficult and had to be done mostly by runners. This made any appreciation of the situation difficult. It certainly did not help, either, that Geyer received over-positive messages from the commanders at the passes during the day. At 1600hrs André reported his men, up to this point,

GERMAN UNITS

Kampfgruppe Schwehr

1 3. Kompanie, Reserve Gebirgsjäger
   Bataillon I/98
2 1. Kompanie, Reserve Gebirgsjäger
   Bataillon I/98
3 7. Kompanie, Reserve Gebirgsjäger
   Bataillon II/98
4 8. Kompanie, Reserve Gebirgsjäger
   Bataillon II/98

FFI UNITS

A Compagnie André

ANDRE

TO ROUSSET

TO COL DE ROUSSET

PAS DES CHATTO

PAS DES BACHASSONS

GRANDE CABANE

PAS DE LA SELLE

MONT AIGU

CHICHILIANNE

TO ST AGNAN-
EN-VERCORS

RÊT DOMANIALE
DU VERCORS

10

A   1   **PAS DE LA BERRIÈVES**

6

PAS DE LA VILLE

1   A

ND VEYMONT

7   6

3

1   **GRESSE-EN-VERCORS**

2

2

3

3

TRÉSANNE

ᴵᴵᴵ
✉ (-)

SCHWEHR

EVENTS

1 Compagnie André deploys around 15 to 20 men at each of the mountain passes to the south-east of the plateau. The company's HQ is located in the shepherd hut of La Grande Cabane.

2 Kampfgruppe Schwehr consists of HQ Reserve Gebirgsjäger-Regiment 1, Reserve Gebirgsjäger Bataillon I/98 and II/98 as well as element of Gebirgs Artillerie Abteilung 79. Oberst Schwehr divides his *Kampfgruppe* into four reinforced companies with machine-gun, mortar and artillery support. Schwehr and his HQ follow the companies of Reserve Gebirgsjäger Bataillon I/98. The commander of Reserve Gebirgsjäger Bataillon II/98, Hauptmann Rességuier de Miremont, attaches himself to his 8. Kompanie.

3 Kampfgruppe Schwehr combs the foothills of the plateau in the morning and early afternoon of 21 July; no contact with the enemy is made.

4 The two companies of Reserve Gebirgsjäger Bataillon II/98 deploy into combat formation beneath the Pas de la Selle and the Pas des Bachassons in the late afternoon.

5 After a short, but intensive fight the French positions at the Pas de la Selle, the Pas des Bachassons and the Pas des Chattons are overrun within two hours. Both companies of Reserve Gebirgsjäger Bataillon II/98 bivouac at their objectives on the passes. The French survivors rout to the interior of the plateau into the Forêt Domaniale du Vercors.

6 The two companies of Reserve Gebirgsjäger Bataillon I/98 fail to take their objectives for the day, the Pas de la Ville and the Pas de Berrièves. It remains unclear whether the Germans pursue these two attacks whole-heartedly.

7 Elements of 7. Kompanie, Reserve Gebirgsjäger Bataillon II/98 climb the Grand Veymont and attack the French positions at the Pas de la Ville from the heights. The Maquis have to withdraw; their resistance virtually ceases on 22 July.

8 Elements of 8. Kompanie, Reserve-Gebirgsjäger-Bataillon II/98 advance over the mountain ridge to the Pas de l'Aiguille in order to defeat remaining Maquisards to the south and secure the *Kampfgruppe's* left flank.

9 At the Pas de l'Aiguille a two-day siege begins. The Germans unsuccessfully try to defeat a group of Maquisards hidden in a cave at the pass. In the night of 23/24 July the French survivors are able to escape to the valley.

10 The Germans take the last of the mountain passes, the Pas de la Berrièves, on 23 July and begin to advance westwards. The search of scattered Maquisards in the Forêt Domaniale du Vercors continues until 25 July when Kampfgruppe Schwehr reaches the villages of Rousset and St Agnan-en-Vercors in the Varnaison valley.

BATTLE FOR THE MOUNTAIN PASSES, 21–23 JULY 1944
German *Gebirgsjäger* charge over the walls of the Vercors fortress

Hauptmann Graf Clemens Rességuier de Miremont (1915–2002), the commander of Reserve Gebirgsjäger Battaillon II/98, which achieved the decisive break-in at the mountain passes on 21 July. An Austrian by birth, Rességuier emigrated to New York after the war and became an artist. (Hammer)

had firmly held their positions against the enemy and inflicted a number of casualties. In reality, the Germans had not yet commenced their major onslaught on the passes when André sent out this message. By the end of the day Geyer was left to understand that all passes were still in French hands.

The next morning on 22 July 7. and 8. Kompanie/Reserve Gebirgsjäger Bataillon II/98, did not immediately exploit their success of the previous day, but consolidated their gains instead; heavy weapons were carried up to the plateau. When the morning fog lifted, a German observation post sitting on one of the mountains surrounding the Pas de la Selle spotted larger enemy troop movements to the south. As this could potentially develop into a threat to Kampfgruppe Schwehr's left flank, 8. Kompanie sent out two platoons. They found a group of Maquisards well entrenched in a cave near the Pas de l'Aiguille. The Officer Commanding 8. Kompanie, Oberleutnant Ritter, hoped to convince them to surrender. Indeed, one Maquisard appeared at the entrance of the cave, his hands raised. However, when Ritter approached him the Maquis opened fire from another cave and wounded Ritter and some of his men. The *Gebirgsjäger* were warned and had to adopt a much more cautious approach. They could rescue their wounded only during the night to transport them back to the Pas de la Selle. On the following day, 23 July, the Germans tried to enfilade the cave with heavy machine guns, mortars and snipers, but all to no avail. The French position seemed impregnable. A real siege of the caves took place for two and a half days. The Germans improvised an explosive charge attached to a rope and swung it from above into the entrance of the cave. The first attempt was unsuccessful; the second killed or wounded some of the 23 Frenchmen hidden inside. Yet the survivors did not surrender, as they knew they would in all likelihood be shot anyway. Their only remaining chance was a surprise breakout. In the night of 23–24 July they dared the impossible. Tiptoeing in the mist past the careless German surveillance posts the Frenchmen miraculously escaped to the valley. For around 60 hours they had held up an entire German company and (with the exception of the fighting at Vassieux) inflicted the largest losses on any single German unit during the entire Vercors battle; 8. Kompanie had suffered four men killed and 14 men wounded during this siege.

In the days immediately after the capture of the first passes 7. Kompanie was more successful than its neighbours from 8. Kompanie. On 22 July it was ordered to roll up the French positions at the passes to the north, where the Maquisards had hitherto warded off all attacks from Reserve Gebirgsjäger Bataillon I/98. First the *Gebirgsjäger* climbed the Grand Veymont, at 2,341m the highest mountain of the Vercors massif. Below them at the Pas de la Ville a handful of Maquisards were still holding out against the attacking forces from the valleys. However, with the Germans now in possession of the dominant high ground above the pass, the French position became untenable. On 22 July the third pass, the Pas de la Ville, thus came under German control. The fourth pass, the Pas de la Berrièves, changed hands on 23 July, but this was merely to secure the German right flank.

It is worth noting that in his regimental orders from 19 July Oberst Schwehr had identified the Pas de la Berrièves as the focus of his main effort for the general attack. However, the rapid success against the passes farther to the south allowed the Germans to change their plans and outflank the French positions. The narrow and steep Pas de la Berrièves and Pas de la Ville no longer had to be taken by frontal attack. This should not conceal the skill of the French defence in this sector, probably favoured by a relatively poor

performance of Reserve Gebirgsjäger Bataillon I/98. Twelve Maquisards had lost their lives at the Pas de la Ville and the Pas de la Berrièves.

By 23/24 July the battle for the passes was over. Although the outcome had already been decided within a few hours on the evening of 21 July by the capture of the Pas de la Selle and the Pas de Chattons, it took the *Gebirgsjäger* another two days to consolidate their gains fully. The French wanted to hold the passes *coûte que coûte* (at all costs). The passes offered a superb natural defence position, but the few Frenchmen were no real match for the German *Gebirgsjäger* supported by heavy weapons. Tired, exhausted and without proper food supplies the surviving Maquisards fled either down into the valley towards Die or withdrew to the east into the huge and dense Forêt Domaniale du Vercors. Here they could have almost indefinitely delayed Kampfgruppe Schwehr's further advance by a series of ambushes, but their morale was broken. The German battle group would suffer no casualties for the rest of the operation in the Vercors. The battle for the passes cost the Germans in all ten men killed and 31 wounded. French figures are difficult to obtain, but they probably totalled between 40 and 50 men killed. It seems the Germans took no prisoners, but shot all captured Maquisards on the spot.

The attack by Kampfgruppe Seeger from the north-east

For both sides it was obvious that the main fighting would take place in the north-east where the road from Grenoble steeply snakes up to the plateau. The entrance gate into St Nizier had already been taken by the Germans in mid-June. From there the landscape changes to the open, wide meadows around Lans-en-Vercors and Villard-de-Lans, framed by two mountain ridges. A small tramway led up to both villages where modest tourism had developed before World War II. The sector was held by 6e BCA under the command of Capitaine Roland Costa de Beauregard ('Durieu'), a *chasseur alpin* like so many other former regular officers in the Vercors.

Interestingly, Generalleutnant Pflaum did not entrust his most experienced regimental commander Oberst Schwehr with the largest *Kampfgruppe* and hence the execution of the main thrust onto the plateau. Instead, Pflaum picked Oberst Alfred Seeger, the commander of Reserve Artillerie Regiment 7. Seeger had just returned from extended sick leave in Germany and had not commanded a *Kampfgruppe* in anti-partisan operations before. He was

LEFT
Gunners of Reserve Gebirgs Artillerie Abteilung 79 on operations at Glières, spring 1944. The mules carry a dismantled mountain howitzer, the Gebirgsgeschütz 36 (7.5cm), which proved effective in the Vercors. (UTM)

RIGHT
Capitaine Roland Costa de Beauregard (1913–2002), the commander of 6e BCA and the northern sector of the Vercors. (UTM)

regarded as rather uncommunicative with sound military leadership skills, but he was far from being an exceptional commander. Furthermore, he was a gunner in the mountain troops and not an infantryman. Seeger's *Kampfgruppe* consisted of Reserve Gebirgsjäger Bataillone 99 and 100, a company of Reserve Pionier Bataillon 7 and one and a half artillery battalions of his own regiment. Parts of the artillery were possibly deployed in an infantry role. The engineer elements attached were supposed to clear the roads of any landmines. In muggy weather during the night of 19–20 July the *Kampfgruppe* marched from Grenoble in the valley up to the fringes of the plateau, bivouacked in the forests and prepared for the coming fight.

At 0430hrs on the morning of 21 July Kampfgruppe Seeger deployed for battle in the line between St Nizier and Engins. Artillery shelled assumed French positions on the plains around Lans. However, when the German *Gebirgsjäger* advanced they met only sporadic opposition. Huet had ordered the area between Lans and Villard to be left largely unmanned, as he rightly understood resistance would be futile in open ground without the support of heavy weapons. Soon after, Kampfgruppe Seeger split up into two sub-groups.

Made up mainly of Reserve Gebirgsjäger Bataillon 100 the smaller first column turned north-westwards to the Col de la Croix-Perrin. Here, 1ère Compagnie/6e BCA under the command of Capitaine André Bordenave ('Dufau'), a former officer in the French colonial troops, tried to block the German advance. However, the 170 Frenchmen of Bordenave's company were no match for the German *Gebirgsjäger*. By infiltrating the fir woods they enveloped the French positions. The Maquis had to withdraw to Autrans, but even there their situation became untenable. At 1700hrs German troops entered the village and shortly after also occupied Méaudre. The understaffed 12e BCA under the command of Henri Ullmann ('Philippe') should have held this sector, but evidently it did not seek to challenge the German penetration and withdrew into the dense forests to the west. The battle for the most northern part of the plateau was over. It did not even last 12 hours.

The second German column comprised the bulk of Kampfgruppe Seeger and pushed over the plain towards Villard. Huet was wise enough to exclude

The fighting in the north, 21–25 July 1944

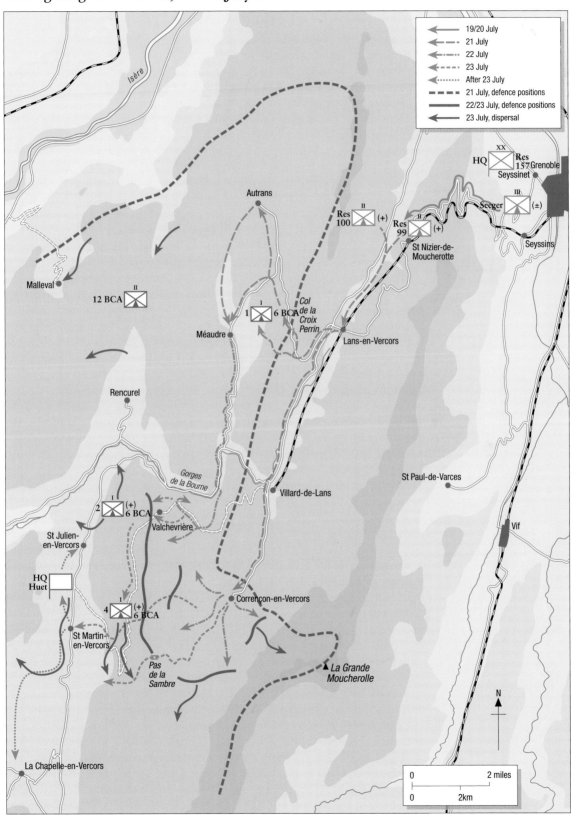

←	19/20 July
←	21 July
←	22 July
←	23 July
←	After 23 July
– – –	21 July, defence positions
——	22/23 July, defence positions
←	23 July, dispersal

Isère

HQ ⊠ XX Res 157 Grenoble
Seyssinet

Res 100 ⊠ II (+)

Seeger ⊠ III (±)

Res 99 ⊠ II (+)

Autrans

St Nizier-de-Moucherotte

Seyssins

Malleval

12 BCA ⊠ II

1 ⊠ I 6 BCA

Col de la Croix Perrin

Méaudre

Lans-en-Vercors

Rencurel

Gorges de la Bourne

Villard-de-Lans

St Paul-de-Varces

2 ⊠ I (+) 6 BCA

Valchevrière

St Julien-en-Vercors

Vif

HQ Huet ☐

4 ⊠ I (+) 6 BCA

Correncon-en-Vercors

St Martin-en-Vercors

Pas de la Sambre

▲ La Grande Moucherolle

N

La Chapelle-en-Vercors

0   2 miles

0   2km

the small spa town from his line of defence as it would have exposed the inhabitants to potential German reprisals. Hence, the Germans reached Villard without a shot and soon marched southwards to Corrençon; their engineers cleared all major roads of mines. At Corrençon the Maquis made a prolonged stand against the Germans. It took the men of Reserve Gebirgsjäger Bataillon 99 about six hours to conquer the village with the support of heavy weapons. Throughout the night the FFI still fired into the settlement from the surrounding hills.

Any further German advance from Corrençon was difficult, as the village was surrounded from all directions by dense forests; this rendered any infiltration time-consuming and orientation very difficult. It was impossible to deploy heavy weapons in this terrain and German troops could easily be trapped in a series of ambushes. The sole proper road leading to the heart of the plateau went through the Gorges de la Bourne, an extremely narrow and deep ravine. The road was mostly blasted out of the rock and interspersed with a series of tunnels and a few bridges all of which the Maquisards had blown up. In summary, the Gorges de la Bourne was not an option for Kampfgruppe Seeger to use for access to the interior of the plateau.

Yet there was another road which could offer a breakthrough into the centre of the Vercors. To the south of the Gorges de la Bourne a small cart path wound along the wooded slopes. Near the abandoned village of Valchevrière, at a place called Belvédère, the road was extremely exposed; Belvédère was a bottleneck the Germans would have to pass through. From there southwards ran the ridge of the Crête de l'Ange extending for about seven kilometres.

Along these natural barriers Huet had defined a continuous line of defence. Overall 400 men were deployed to this area; they came from the 2e and 4e Compagnie/6e BCA reinforced by a platoon from the 12e BCA and a detachment of black Tirailleurs Sénégalais, former French colonial soldiers who had fled from German captivity. The overall commander of this force was Jean Prévost.

The FFI had blocked the road to Belvédère with trees and mines. Prévost had entrusted his most experienced commander with the defence of this vital ground: Lieutenant Abel Chabal, a full-blooded soldier. Born to poor mountain farmers in 1910 he had not been able to pursue an academic career, but enlisted in the army as an NCO instead. After service in the colonies he transferred to 6e BCA. In 1943 Chabal joined the Resistance and came to the Vercors in February 1944 where he became a military instructor. During the first action at St Nizier on 13 June Chabal excelled by carrying out the decisive counter-attack with his platoon. Descour granted him a commission for this feat of arms. It must have been an emotional moment for Chabal when his old 6e BCA was reconstituted in the Vercors and he now served in it as an officer. He was definitely a good choice to command the defence at Belvédère.

Chabal deployed the first platoon up front to overlook the minefields, the second platoon directly along the road at the Belvédère bottleneck and the third platoon on the heights to the south. The fourth platoon remained in Valchevrière as a reserve. His plan was certainly reasonable and his men motivated. Armed with Stens, Brens, Lee-Enfields and bazookas they were certainly better equipped than the average Vercors company. However, like almost all other units, they lacked experience and training. Although the 92 men of Chabal's company could rely on a terrain that massively favoured the defender, the prospect of success was rather bleak.

Kampfgruppe Seeger remained rather hesitant on the second day of the Vercors battle. After its swift success on the first day of the operation, Seeger ordered a much more cautious approach. This was sensible as the wooded terrain just did not allow large-scale manoeuvres. Yet the *Gebirgsjäger* did not remain inactive, and sent out numerous reconnaissance patrols to the forests and mountains around Corrençon. The results allowed Seeger to obtain a relatively clear picture of the enemy.

One of these patrols met Chabal's men at Belvédère and the French warded off the *Gebirgsjäger*. As a consequence, Prévost sent an enthusiastic telegram to Huet: 'Success at Valchevrière. Chabal repulses the enemy and inflicts severe casualties.' In contrast, the German casualty records do not mention a single loss. Once again Huet received an exaggerated message from one of his subordinates which made it difficult to obtain a reliable picture of the situation.

Overall, the second day of the battle was not as disastrous as the first for the French. At Vassieux the German parachutists were isolated; in the south the Germans had not yet attempted to attack the plateau from the Drôme Valley; at the passes in the south-east the enemy had not exploited their initial success and neither had they made any gains on 22 July in the north-east. However, Huet and the vast majority of the other leaders knew that this was just the calm before the storm. In particular, Kampfgruppe Seeger would soon launch an all-out attack at Valchevrière.

THE PURSUIT

Nowhere had the FFI been able to stop the German advance during the first 48 hours of battle. Some units displayed outstanding bravery, but open fighting turned out to be a full-scale disaster from the start. Already on the evening of 21 July, Huet convened a meeting in his headquarters at the Villa Bellon in St Martin-en-Vercors. Almost all key military commanders and civilian leaders attended, amongst them Zeller, Huet, his assistant René Bousquet ('Chabert'), his chief of staff Pierre Tanant ('Laroche'), Cammaerts,

LEFT
It would be wrong to believe only the French fought in the FFI. Having escaped from German prisoner of war camps a platoon consisting of *Tirailleurs Sénégalais* fought for the Maquis du Vercors in the sector near Valchevrière. (MRV)

RIGHT
Jean Prévost (1901–1944) played a crucial role as a company commander in the engagements at St Nizier on 13–15 June and at Belvédère on 22–23 July. A novelist by profession, Prévost joined the Resistance because of his deep republican conviction. (IWM)

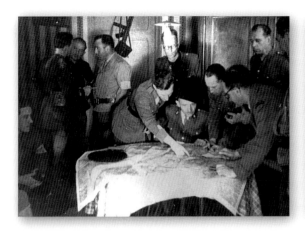 

Chavant and Longe. As usual, Longe needed the assistance of his translator Paray to follow the conversation.

Smoking a cigarette Huet calmly outlined the serious situation his FFI forces were in: 'We have to look at things as they are; unless a miracle happens, our lines will collapse; after tomorrow or the following day, it will be impossible for us to oppose the Germans with any coherent resistance. We have only one solution left; we must disperse.' Cold silence fell on the room. Nobody had expected Huet to give in so quickly. Bousquet was the first to raise his voice. He suggested all remaining troops should withdraw from their defences, concentrate in the heart of the plateau and finally, as a marching column, fight their way through into the Drôme area to the south of the plateau. Zeller, Chavant and Cammaerts approved this idea.

However, in the end Huet convinced them of the impossibility of organizing a fighting withdrawal with such an inexperienced force as the Maquis du Vercors. Besides, the Germans had already broken through the French defence in the Drôme Valley and approached Die. A potential line of retreat to the south was hence cut off. Eventually it was decided to disperse within the plateau. The large forests, in particular the Forêt de Lente in the west, offered numerous hideouts which would allow the Maquisards to hold out for a couple of days until the Germans withdrew. Zeller and Cammaerts chose to leave the plateau as they held military responsibilities for a wider geographical area than just the Vercors. Runners distributed the dispersal order to various units on the plateau on the day after the fateful conference. However, the troops still had to wait until Huet authorized the execution of the order. It would be given only once the whole defence had collapsed.

As seen, 22 July indeed gave the FFI a glimmer of hope that things might not turn into the most extreme disaster. On this day German progress was very slow in the south, at the passes and in the north-east; furthermore, the *Fallschirmjäger* might still be contained at Vassieux. However, on the following day all optimism burst like a balloon. With the exception of the passes, the Germans would go on to achieve a decisive breakthrough at all three other fronts.

To the south of the plateau Kampfgruppe Zabel had rested on 22 July; it cleared the area around Die and prepared for the major attack onto the plateau. The *Kampfgruppe* was only 15km away as the crow flies from the besieged *Fallschirmjäger* at Vassieux, but between them lay a mountain pass, the Col du Rousset. It was the obvious axis of advance for the armoured column of the battle group. A seemingly endless serpentine road leads up the

steep slopes; this road, however, does not traverse the summit of the pass, but passes through a tunnel about 150 metres below. Here, the Maquisards had hidden a number of supplies from the air drops of 14 July. There was no question of letting the cache fall into German hands. A race against time started; could the FFI evacuate the tunnel and blow it up before the Germans arrived? In the end, the French won. Just as the *Panzergrenadiere*'s first vehicles approached the tunnel, a massive detonation could be heard above the valley; the road from Die to Vassieux was blocked. It was one of the last minor tactical victories for the French Resistance before the final collapse. Kampfgruppe Zabel was hence unable to push towards Vassieux over the Col du Rousset, but had to move on foot over the Col de Vassieux instead – a time-consuming mission given the mountainous and wooded terrain.

Although the *Fallschirmjäger* of Kampfgruppe Schäfer still had to wait to be relieved by ground forces in the ruins of Vassieux, their situation improved considerably during 23 July. On this day the skies finally cleared again and the Luftwaffe could support the paratroopers as it pleased. Already at 0725hrs in the morning another 20 DFS 230s gliders from I./LLG 1 landed near the village bringing in desperately needed reinforcements. Amongst them were 50 men from an eastern battalion. Their exact unit remains uncertain, but their actions were well documented. In an almost inexplicable rage these men killed Resistance fighters and civilians alike in the village and the surrounding hamlets. In addition, 20 more French collaborators (possibly from the Brandenburgers) with specialist knowledge of the Resistance joined the *Fallschirmjäger*. Unusually two Gotha Go 242A gliders from I./LLG 2 landed on the same day; another followed on 24 July. The Go 242A was an enhanced version of the DFS 230 with about double the capacity. As it could also transport larger cargo, heavy support weapons could finally be flown in. An anti-aircraft gun was set up on the slopes to the west of Vassieux, where it dominated the ground uncontested and could support Schäfer's men. In addition, a Fi 156 (Fieseler Storch) and later even a Ju 52 landed on the road between Vassieux and La Mure and at the Taille-Crayon airstrip; they evacuated the wounded, amongst them SS-Obersturmbannführer Werner Knab. Completely unharmed by Allied aircraft the fighter-bombers of Kampfgeschwader Bongart – joined by planes from Jagdführer (Jafü) Süd – relentlessly hammered the French positions surrounding Vassieux. By 24 July the ring of besieging forces was nothing more than a thin screen. In this overall context it hardly mattered that the Germans had lost four DFS 230s on 23 July; three had landed or crashed miles away from Vassieux, a fourth fatally hit a power cable near the village.

LEFT
Men of the 11e Régiment de Cuirassiers on exercise near the mountain passes on the southern edge of the plateau a few days prior to the German onslaught on 21 July 1944. (MRV)

RIGHT
One of the three Go 242s which landed at Vassieux on 23–24 July 1944. It transported some of the heavy weapons so desperately needed by Kampfgruppe Schäfer. The Go 242 saw only limited operational action during the war. (MRV)

In the north, Kampfgruppe Seeger took up the offensive again at 0500hrs on 23 July. Its last obstacle was the French position at Belvédère and Valchevrière defended by the 92 men of Chabal's company. At dawn the first German *Gebirgsjäger* cautiously approached the Belvédère bottleneck before they came under small arms fire. What followed was a classic example of an attack in mountain terrain, a manoeuvre any *Gebirgsjäger* officer would have learned right from the start of his career; the first men being shot at sought cover, returned fire with the support of mortars, and hence fixed the enemy. The following troops penetrated the dense forest and outflanked the French forces over the slopes. When Chabal saw a number of *Gebirgsjäger* on the heights above his troops, he ordered a counter-attack; his superior Prévost promised to send reinforcements. But outnumbered, the French defence quickly crumbled.

Chabal's last message to Prévost has often been cited as an emotional example of the Maquis's courage and patriotism: 'I am almost completely encircled. We prepare for a Sidi-Brahim. Long live France!' Sidi-Brahim was a battle in Algeria in 1845 where French *chasseurs* had fought against a much larger number of Arabs and were killed almost to the last man. The name of the battle had since become a code of honour and a synonym for ultimate self-sacrifice within the French *chasseurs*. So Belvédère was a Sidi-Brahim in the Vercors; Chabal was mortally wounded at 1100hrs, his men killed or fleeing. The Germans set on fire the village of Valchevrière, which had been deserted for several years. Some hours later in the afternoon the Germans also crossed the Col de la Sambue. The last line of defence for the interior of the plateau had collapsed and the fate of the Maquis du Vercors was now finally sealed.

When Huet learned about the defeat at Belvédère his last glimmer of hope vanished; the game was over. He did not hesitate a minute in ordering the execution of his dispersal order at 1600hrs on 23 July. All French detainees and the handful of German prisoners were released. Huet wanted to show his enemy that his forces were not 'terrorists', but part of a regular army. Standing on the balcony of his headquarters in St Martin for the last time he saw German artillery shells hitting the village and its surroundings. Then he fled with some men of his staff on the road over Barraques and reached the Forêt de Lente in the next few days.

Between 21 and 23 July the French had sent numerous telegrams to London and to Algiers. All requested the same things: Allied air support and a bombardment of Chabeuil airfield to prevent German air supremacy over the Vercors. But nothing happened. The telegrams either remained unanswered or the response to them was kept vague. Not until 24 July did 60 B-24s of 15th USAAF attack Chabeuil airfield and destroy or badly damage 24 German aircraft on the ground. Further sporadic Allied air raids followed in the coming days, but it was far too late to have any impact on the course of the operation.

To the present day the reason why the Allies and de Gaulle had denied any tangible support to the FFI on the Vercors plateau has remained a highly controversial topic. The surviving documents do not provide us with a satisfactory answer. After the war various claims were made that de Gaulle had betrayed his countrymen. He looked away when the Maquis du Vercors was destroyed – a Maquis which may have become politically too powerful. Yet this Maquis was predominantly Gaullist and it is difficult to imagine the general would have wished that his own supporters lose this battle. As a result, this would have meant giving political ground to the communist Resistance movement. When considering the lack of Allied support for the FFI in the Vercors one must acknowledge the facts; no one in London or Algiers had authorized a general mobilization of the forces on the plateau. The Allies had made clear that they could not support the Maquis du Vercors for the time being, as the instruction orders of mission 'Eucalyptus' explicitly stated. The earlier Plan Montagnard was never agreed. At the same time the Normandy battle was reaching its climax and furthermore US and Free French forces were preparing for an imminent major landing on the Mediterranean coast in southern France. The priorities of Allied military planners probably lay elsewhere during these days and weeks. The Maquis du Vercors had to carry the can themselves.

This did not of course alter the frustration and rage of the men on the plateau. Chavant's famous message to Algiers in the night of 21–22 July perfectly exemplified this sentiment: 'Morale of the population excellent, but will turn rapidly against you, if you do not take immediate dispositions and we agree with them in saying that those in London and Algiers have understood nothing about the situation we are in. These men [in London and Algiers] are considered criminals and cowards. Indeed, criminals and cowards.' It was an angry and desperate cry for help – but to no avail.

A shocking photo of Maquisards, hanged at La Mure. *Fallschirmjäger* and eastern troops behaved with utmost brutality towards FFI and civilians alike around Vassieux. The atrocities these units committed exceeded, by far, those of any other German units in the Vercors. (MRV)

Even after the French forces dispersed in small groups the Germans still advanced cautiously. Not until the morning of 25 July did Zabel's *Panzergrenadiere* finally relieve the *Fallschirmjäger* in Vassieux. Together they cleared the area around the village for which both sides had fought so fiercely in the past five days. In a speedy advance, the men of Kampfgruppe Zabel moved on to St Martin and reached the rural community on 26 July. The paratroopers of Kampfgruppe Schäfer marched northwards, too, but remained at La Chapelle. Many books on the Vercors wrongly claim the *Gebirgsjäger* of Kampfgruppe Schwehr linked up with the airborne forces at Vassieux. This is wrong however; German documents clearly show that it took Schwehr's *Gebirgsjäger* three days to march from the passes in the south-east over the plateau. On 25 July the two battalions of Kampfgruppe Schwehr reached the line St Agnan–Rousset.

THE MOPPING-UP PHASE

Strictly speaking the military operations terminated with the relief of the *Fallschirmjäger* in Vassieux on 25 July. However, this did not constitute the end of the entire operation. Over the following ten days the Germans searched thoroughly for the dispersed men of the former Maquis du Vercors. At the same time the civilian population on and around the plateau became subject to harsh German reprisals.

Already during the military phase the Germans had acted ruthlessly, if not brutally, on many occasions. Kampfgruppe Zabel had killed a number of French civilians on its advance in the Drôme Valley. Men of Kampfgruppe Schäfer displayed particularly vicious behaviour during the five days of fighting around Vassieux. The village lay in ruins; 72 civilians, amongst them women and children, had lost their lives during the air bombardments or at the hands of the *Fallschirmjäger*. The Eastern troops ransacked the neighbouring hamlets and murdered inhabitants in the most atrocious way. On its march back to Grenoble Kampfgruppe Schäfer burned all farmhouses along the road between Vassieux and La Chapelle, where they met men of Kampfgruppe Seeger on the afternoon of 25 July. The Germans set large parts of La Chapelle on fire and shot 16 hostages. They considered the village to be a former FFI headquarters. The following morning Kampfgruppe Schäfer marched down to the valley. For these men the Vercors operation was over.

When Schäfer personally reported to his superior, Oberst Heigl, he was also questioned whether his men had participated in any atrocities. Schäfer bluntly lied and denied all claims; his superiors willingly believed him and he was awarded the Knight's Cross for the leadership of his *Kampfgruppe* and the personal bravery he had displayed when his men fought in isolation in Vassieux. Originally Schäfer's unit was to have been deployed again straight away in another daring mission. The men of KG 200 had been intended to land behind US lines and take the bridge at Avranches from where the US Army had broken out of the Normandy front in early August. With the rapid collapse of the German defence in Normandy, however, this project never materialized.

Kampfgruppe Zabel, too, was withdrawn from the plateau on 26 July and moved back southwards into the Drôme Valley. Probably on the same day, the three key German personalities responsible for this operation visited the plateau; the overall commander Niehoff (Commander of Army Area

Southern France), Pflaum and finally Knab who had recovered reasonably well from wounds inflicted during the fight at Vassieux. Allegedly, Niehoff and Knab reproved Pflaum. Both believed Pflaum's 157. Reserve Division had acted too moderately. In fact, the FFI reported that the Germans were 'pitiless against the Maquisards and their supporters', but at the same time had by large behaved 'correctly' towards the rest of the population.

On 27 July Niehoff ordered the systematic mopping-up of the plateau and its environs. The aim was to 'render any future re-forming of the enemy impossible in the Vercors'. The Germans did not have the men to occupy the plateau permanently in order to adopt a 'clear–hold–build' strategy. It was a full-on 'search-and-destroy' mission instead. This meant the Maquis would be deprived of its means of survival. The male population between 17 and 30 years were to be arrested and grouped into work detachments, even if those men had never had anything to do with the Maquis. Private and public houses which had accommodated the 'terrorists' were to be burnt. Exceptions were to be made if the inhabitants had been forced to lodge the Maquis. All livestock was to be taken away from the local farmers and they would be allowed to keep only the absolute minimum for survival. Depending on the size of the family, this normally meant two to three cows and a calf each, plus all small livestock and poultry. After the operation the German military administration counted 700 head of cattle driven down into the valley. As there were no means of transport, the animals had to be slaughtered. Meat of lower quality was handed over to the French civilian population around Grenoble, the rest requisitioned by 157. Reserve Division.

The mopping-up phase lasted even longer than the actual military phase of the operation. Between 27 July and 5 August Seeger's and Schwehr's *Gebirgsjäger* stayed on the plateau; each of the four battalions was allocated a sector to search for Maquisards and carry out reprisals. The troops around the plateau did the same by tightening the ring of encirclement, particularly in the west. To the south elements of Kampfgruppe Zabel sought to penetrate remote side valleys of the Drôme, where some of the last organized Maquis groups had survived the huge German offensive. At Gigors on 27 July the FFI were even successful in repelling half-hearted German attempts to penetrate deeper into the valleys, even though the Luftwaffe provided close air support. The *Panzergrenadiere* lost five men wounded and then withdrew. These were the last military actions of the Vercors operation.

On the plateau a manhunt started. The Vercors has few sources of water. Hence the Germans put guards near these sources; they correctly expected scattered Maquisards would have to assuage their thirst in the hot summer days sooner or later. If caught, FFI members were mostly shot on the spot or in some rare cases transferred to SD prison cells. Sometimes the prisoners were herded together and executed en masse after a short trial as in St-Nazaire-en-Royans. The Milice also took part in these killings. The Germans did not even spare the life of wounded personnel. *Gebirgsjäger* of Kampfgruppe Schwehr discovered a hospital in the Grotte de la Luire on 27 July, probably after a young local boy had divulged the hideout. The nurses were deported to Ravensbrück concentration camp in Germany. Only one doctor and US Lieutenant Myers of OG 'Justine' were spared, even though the latter should have been killed according to the infamous central 'Commando Order' of 1942.

The Germans denied all access to the plateau to representatives of the French administration, the Red Cross or the Secours National. The prefect of Isère, Philippe Frantz, protested energetically, but in vain, against this restrictive policy, although he was himself considered a Fascist and thus killed by the Resistance only a few days later. In many cases the locals were even prohibited from burying the bodies of fallen or shot Maquisards; their cadavers rotted in the sun. Yet, in all this violence, there were still some acts of humanity. After the war the priest of Vassieux declared that in certain cases *Gebirgsjäger* units combing the area had left the civilian population unharmed and even treated some of the wounded FFI. The village of St Martin, where Huet had had his headquarters, largely escaped the flames thanks to the personal intervention of a senior *Gebirgsjäger* officer.

The majority of the Resistance fighters withdrew in small groups into the dense Forêt de Lente in the west of the plateau. Amongst them were the key commanders Huet and Geyer as well as OG 'Justine'. De Beauregard withdrew to the forests around Autrans in the far north of the plateau. The more skilful officers were able to maintain the core cohesion within their units and many of these formations made it to the Forêt de Lente. However, a good number of Maquisards had not received Huet's dispersal order and tried to survive by hiding out in other areas of the Vercors or tried to break through the encirclement ring. They often became easy prey for German patrols and were shot on the spot. Prévost was killed in an attempt to reach Sassenage on 1 August.

The two British majors of mission 'Eucalyptus' took a different route. Without contact with any FFI commanders, hampered by their limited French language skills, and plagued by unbearable thirst Longe and Houseman initially wandered around in the forests near St Martin for a few days. Then they sneaked through the encirclement ring to the north of the plateau near La Rivière and fled to Switzerland, where they were interned. Shortly after their return to the United Kingdom in September 1944 Longe and Houseman had to face a court of inquiry to establish whether their flight to Switzerland was an act of cowardice and whether the 'conduct of these officers was in accordance with the traditions of the British Army'. In the end the court acquitted both and they were awarded the Military Cross for bravery in May 1945.

On 5 August the last *Gebirgsjäger* descended from the plateau after 16 days on operations. The Germans left the land devastated; the combat and the following reprisals had affected almost every community on and around the Vercors plateau; over 500 houses were destroyed, the villages of Vassieux and La Chapelle were laid waste. The death toll on both sides was much heavier than in any other German anti-partisan operation in France during the war. The Germans lost 65 men killed, 133 wounded and another 18 missing with the biggest casualty numbers occurring in Kampfgruppe Schäfer. On the French side the FFI deplored the loss of life of 639 of their men; furthermore, 201 civilian victims were reported dead with a good number of them from Vassieux. These are the numbers for the plateau based on a calculation the US Intelligence Officer Peter H. Nash made after a visit to the Vercors in 1945. Exact numbers for the area around the mountain massif are still missing today. The Vercors had ceased to be the largest centre of resistance in occupied France. However, the German success was only short-lived. The vast majority of the Maquisards had either managed to hide out in the Forêt de Lente or sneaked through the encirclement ring. All of their major leaders had survived. Huet and many of his men lived to fight another day.

THE TARENTAISE

After the operations in the Vercors had ended 157. Reserve Division did not get a respite. The Maquis had now become a real danger to German troops; large parts of the region were in turmoil against the occupier and the dying Vichy regime, which was unable to maintain its authority. Controlling all the Alpine valleys was impossible in this situation but, at the least, the key major roads leading from the Rhône Valley to the French–Italian border had to be kept open and secured. Given the collapse of the Normandy front in early August, a retreat from southern France seemed imminent, all the more so as a second Allied landing was expected. Under these circumstances the Kommandant des Heeresgebiets Südfrankreich ordered a new series of operations in the French Alps all under the codename *Hochsommer* (Midsummer). The first areas to be cleared simultaneously were the Romanche Valley east of Grenoble and the Tarentaise Valley between Albertville and the Little Saint Bernard Pass.

To attack the Maquis forces in the Romanche area Pflaum had amassed 3,000 to 4,000 men, mainly from his division, and organized in four *Kampfgruppen* which would meet in the area of Bourg d'Oisans, a small market town in the heart of the Romanche Valley. The operation meant a

A German officer instructs Turkmene troops by a sandpit model, northern France late 1943. In all likelihood these men belonged to the Ostbataillon (Turk) 781, which was transferred to southern France in summer 1944 for anti-partisan operations. It took part in the operation *Hochsommer* near Briançon. (BA, 101I-295-1561-04)

further radicalization of 157. Reserve Division's anti-partisan policy. This time the entire male population between 16 and 55 years of age was to be deported to Germany for labour, regardless of whether they had previously supported the Maquis or not. Furthermore, the Germans combined this military operation with a quest for raw materials stored in the area such as aluminium, magnesium, electrum or carbide. Recovery teams of Feldwirtschaftskommando 9 accompanied the individual battle groups. This commando was also to confiscate all cars, ski equipment and radios. Military and economic considerations went hand in hand in this operation against the Maquis. Up to this point not a single German soldier had ever set foot in the Romanche Valley.

This large operation started on 8 August, but ended inconclusively. Le Ray, the commander of the FFI in this area, ordered an immediate withdrawal to the interior of the valley or to the heights of the mountains. Bearing in mind the cruel fate of his colleagues in the Vercors he had learned the lesson that his poorly armed forces could not fight a prolonged battle against the Germans, but could only apply purely guerilla-style hit-and-run tactics. The only two significant engagements took place on 9 August after a Maquis ambush near La Mure, and around 15 August when the Maquis defended some of their positions in the mountains near L'Alpe (today one of the largest ski resorts in France). Le Ray also ordered his men to stay away from villages as far as possible so that the local population was not exposed to German reprisals. Indeed, the Germans behaved less brutally than in the Vercors. Yet, there were bloody exceptions to the rule. Coming from Briançon, two companies of Ostbataillon 781 left a trail of blood on their march. At the Col du Lautaret they executed more than a dozen mountain farmers on 11 August and later ransacked the villages of La Grave and Villar-d'Arène. Furthermore, the Sipo/SD shot eight hostages in Bourg d'Oisans on 14 and 15 August, some of them Jews and foreigners. Overall, German casualties stood at about 15 killed or wounded in action in this operation; French losses totalled about 30. The Germans finally called off Operation *Hochsommer* in the Romanche Valley on 17 August, i.e. two days after the

A flare signal prepared for Allied container night drops in the Savoie, spring 1944. It was not until summer 1944 that the Allied air power dared to fly day missions in support of the French Resistance. (IWM)

Members of the Inter-Allied Mission 'Union II', all exclusively recruited from the USMC. These men were some of the very few US Marines who served in Europe during World War II. (UTM)

Allied landings in southern France. Neither the interned male population nor the raw materials could be removed, owing to lack of transport.

The second part of *Hochsommer* took place in the Tarentaise, the mountain valley along the upper course of the Isère River. An important route to Italy ran through the valley. Moreover, there was heavy industry there, particularly around Moûtiers, Pomblière and La Léchère. The Germans knew about the significance of the Tarentaise and thus had always kept a strong garrison in Albertville with Reserve Gebirgs Artillerie Abteilung 79 and Reserve Gebirgsjäger Bataillon 100 in Bourg-St-Maurice and Moûtiers. Smaller detachments lay along the valley. The 1. Kompanie/SS-Polizei Regiment 19 was also present in the area around Albertville. Right up to D-Day this part of Savoie was deemed relatively calm and this did not initially change after 6 June. Nevertheless, immediately after D-Day the local French Resistance forces carried out a few ambushes on German columns such as at the Etroit de Siaix tunnel near St Marcel where Reserve Gebirgsjäger Bataillon 100 lost one man killed and another nine wounded. However, the FFI soon had to realize that the support of the local population was rather limited in the Tarentaise and other parts of Savoie owing to fear of German reprisals. In fact, elements of SS-Polizei Regiment 19 executed 27 randomly selected civilians on 5 June after some of their men fell victim to an FTPF ambush near Ugine. But above all, the FFI lacked arms. Out of 2,000 mobilized men only 400 could be armed. Setbacks were unavoidable, such as the denunciation of the FTPF leader of the Tarentaise, Claudius Poux; the Germans tortured and executed him on 15 June. Consequently, the Maquisards's morale collapsed; they dispersed and returned to their homes by mid-June.

Only a small core was left which retreated to the Beaufortain, where the Maquis cut off all access; during the last week of June the Germans penetrated the area and inflicted casualties on the FFI, but withdrew again instantly. They did not have the manpower to hold this remote area. The Beaufortain served as a safe haven and the FFI commanders – above all Capitaine Bulle – planned a second mobilization of the area. As in most parts of the French Alps the Gaullist AS was clearly the dominant political force behind the Resistance movement in Savoie. Yet, owing to the heavy industry in the Tarentaise Valley, the communist FTPF found more supporters here than in most other parts of the Alps.

On 1 August the situation changed fundamentally and the FFI became a force to reckon with; in Operation *Buick*, 195 US Army Air Force planes dropped large quantities of supplies to the Maquis in France. The main target was the Col de Saisies in Savoie. It was the largest airdrop ever to be carried out in occupied France: 1,350 rifles, 1,096 Sten guns, 260 pistols, 298 Bren guns, 51 anti-tank weapons, 1,030 hand grenades and large quantities of explosives – enough to arm around 3,000 men in the Savoie region. To the Maquis's disappointment, however, no heavy weapons and transmitters were dropped. Bulle organized the distribution of the weapons; the majority went to the Resistance groups in the Beaufortain and the Tarentaise. The Inter-Allied Mission 'Union II' parachuted in at the Col de Saisies, too. Commanded by USMC Major Peter J. Ortiz it consisted of seven members of the US Marine Corps, a Frenchman and the British Major Thackwaite ('Procureur'). Unfortunately, one of the members, Sergeant Charles Perry, died in the drop, as his parachute did not open.

The arrival of the new supplies was timely, as in early August the vast majority of the local German troops were still deployed in the Vercors. Instead of two battalions only two reinforced companies were available to secure the garrisons and communication lines in the Tartentaise Valley – not enough to maintain order, as the events of the following days revealed. On 4 August a German column tried to climb the Cormet d'Arêches, one of the mountain passes linking the Beaufortain and the Tarentaise, in order to prevent the Maquis from trafficking arms. However, the FFI repulsed the Germans at the hamlet of Laval; three Germans were killed and two wounded. This was just a precursor of things to come; between 5 and 8 August the Maquisards liberated the entire Tarentaise Valley. The remnants of Reserve Gebirgsjäger Bataillon 100 alone lost 12 men killed and 24 wounded, and 45 were taken prisoner. The 157. Reserve Division had never experienced such a high number of losses during any operation against the Maquis. French casualties were relatively light with about a dozen killed. The German garrison of Bourg-St-Maurice had to withdraw to the Little St Bernard Pass and hence the communication lines to Italy were broken. Previously, the FFI had mostly shot their German prisoners, but now Bulle ordered that they be treated according to the Geneva Convention. Furthermore, the FFI agreed a truce with the German commander of the forces at the Little St Bernard Pass, Oberleutnant Otmar Wirth. Joy about the liberation initially reigned amongst the local people, but the relationship between them and the Maquis was fragile. Bulle reacted by replacing two of the sub-sector commanders in the Tarentaise who had not gained full acceptance amongst the people. The key problem still remained; Maquisards and civilians alike feared harsh reprisals should the Germans reconquer the valley. And they were completely isolated from outside help because the awaited Allied landing in southern France had not started yet. As a consequence morale was falling amongst the Maquis, since they sensed the liberation of the Tarentaise may have been a premature act.

The German reaction was not long in the waiting. Reserve Gebirgsjäger Bataillon 100, Reserve Grenadier Bataillon 179, and elements of Reserve Gebirgs Artillerie Abteilung 79 rushed back from the operation in the Vercors and rallied at Albertville. They were possibly accompanied by some Sipo/SD personnel. The German force counted around 1,500 to 1,800 men and was commanded by Major Johann Kolb, one of 157. Reserve Division's most highly decorated officers. The mission was obvious: the relief of their beleaguered colleagues at the Little St Bernard Pass and the restoration of

GERMAN UNITS
1 Reserve Grenadier Bataillon 179
2 Reserve Gebirgsjäger Bataillon 100
3 Reserve Gebirgs Artillerie Abteilung 79
4 II./SS-Polizei Regiment 15

FFI UNITS
A FFI forces
B Inter-Allied Mission 'Union II'
C FFI Compagnie du Lac

ALBERTVILLE
COL DE LA BÂTHIE
NÂVES   COL DE LA LOUZE
FEISSONS-SUR-ISÈRE
CEVINS
PUSSY
MONTGIROD
AIGUEBLANCHE
CENTRON
NOTRE-DAME-DU-PRÉ
LONG
MOÛTIERS
LA PLA

Regiment
z.b.v. Kolb   ⊠ (-)
KOLB

▼ **EVENTS**

1 1 August: almost 1,000 containers are dropped by the USAAF at the Col des Saisies allowing the entire FFI in the Beaufortain area to be armed. The Interallied Mission 'Union II' with USMC Major Peter J. Ortiz is also parachuted at the same location in order to liaise with local FFI forces.

2 6/7 August: the local FFI attack the remainder of the German garrisons in Bourg-St-Maurice and Moûtiers. The first one withdraws to the Little St Bernard Pass, the latter one capitulates. II./SS-Polizei Regiment 15 reinforces the garrison at the Little St Bernard Pass from Aosta in Italy.

3 Before 10 August: the FFI prepare a series of consecutive ambushes at natural barriers in the Tarentaise valley to counter the expected German offensive.

4 10 August: Reserve Grenadier Bataillon 179, Reserve Gebirgsjäger Bataillon 100 and elements of Reserve Gebirgs Artillerie Abteilung 79 launch the large German counter-offensive in the Tarentaise. The reconnaissance elements meet their first opposition near Feissons-sur-Isère around 0900hrs.

5 10 August: whilst Reserve Grenadier Bataillon 179 fixes the FFI in the valley, the companies of Reserve Gebirgsjäger Bataillon 100 outflank the enemy forces over the steep slopes above Feissons to either side of the valley. As a consequence the French resistance crumbles quickly. The village of Pussy is partly burnt by the Germans.

6 11 August: the commander of the local FFI, Capitaine Jean Bulle, decides to throw his reserve, the Compagnie du Lac, into the battle. Due to the unclear tactical situation in the valley the company, however, does not engage in the fight until 14 August.

7 11–13 August: after the breakthrough north of Aigueblanche, German troops pursue the fleeing FFI. On 13 August the Germans capture Moûtiers again and also the last natural barrier, the Etroit de Siaix.

8 14 August: skirmish at Montgirod. The Compagnie du Lac prevents encirclement against three German companies and withdraws with other scattered forces to the Cormet d'Arêches. Other FFI units dissolve and most Maquisards go back home. The Germans torch Montgirod after the battle in retaliation.

9 15–16 August: without meeting major resistance the Germans advance to Bourg-St-Maurice. The isolated German garrison at the Little St Bernard Pass is relieved and descends to the town again. At the same time weak elements of Reserve Gebirgsjäger Bataillon 100 fail to penetrate at the Cormet d'Arêches.

10 16 August: Major Ortiz and some other members of mission 'Union II' are taken prisoner at Centron after a short fight in the village.

11 21 August: elements of Reserve Gebirgsjäger Bataillon 100 advance into the Chapieux Valley to remove the threat in the flanks of the Tarentaise Valley. However, the Compagnie du Lac and other FFI forces frustrate all these attempts.

THE TARENTAISE, AUGUST 1944
The Germans end the short-lived first liberation of the valley

Note: Gridlines are shown at intervals of 5km/3.10miles

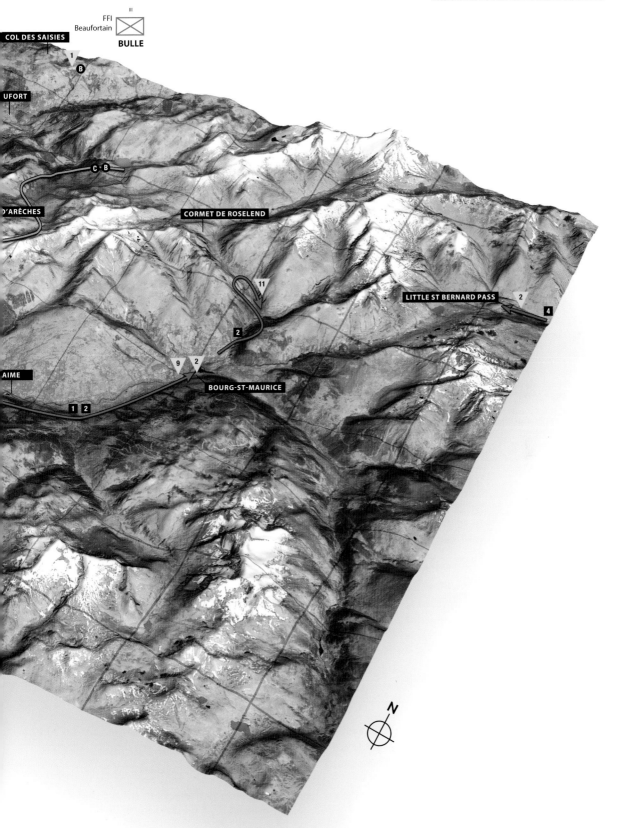

FFI
Beaufortain
BULLE

COL DES SAISIES
UFORT
D'ARÈCHES
CORMET DE ROSELEND
LITTLE ST BERNARD PASS
BOURG-ST-MAURICE
AIME

77

USMC Major Ortiz and the commander of the FFI forces in the Beaufortain, Capitaine Jean-Marie Bulle (with glasses), inspect FFI forces at the Col de la Forclaz near Ugine on 7 August. The French Resistance had just liberated the neighbouring Tarentaise and the Beaufortain served as a safe haven. (UTM)

German authority in the Tarentaise. To this end II./SS-Polizei Regiment 15 was to join the operation from the Aosta Valley in Italy and support the garrison at the Little St Bernard Pass.

Bulle and the other local Resistance commanders knew that the Germans would outclass them in battle. Yet they made the same mistake as their colleagues in the Vercors earlier; relying on favourable terrain they hoped to hold the ground and ward off the enemy. They chose to set up a series of four blocking positions at the narrowest points of the Tarentaise Valley: the first between Cevins and Feissons-sur-Isère, the second between Feissons and Notre-Dame-de-Briançon, the third just before Moûtiers and the fourth and last one at the Etroit du Siaix. This defence plan contained a disastrous geographical split in the areas of responsibility; whilst the Gaullist AS was in charge of the region to the right bank of the Isère River, the Communist FTPF assumed responsibility for the left bank. This would have required excellent coordination in defending the barrages in the valley, but cooperation between both Resistance movements had never been satisfactory.

On 9 August the Germans dispatched reconnaissance parties from Albertville to the first villages in the Lower Tarentaise. Opposition was weak and on the following day the main German attack commenced. A cyclist platoon from Reserve Grenadier Bataillon 179 spearheaded the column. They passed Cevins where Bulle had planned his first barrage. However, the defence was ill-coordinated, as some Maquis groups just did not show up. The first contact happened just before Feissons. After a few shots and some light casualties, the Germans withdrew. The Maquisards celebrated what they considered to be a first victory. However, this was fundamentally wrong and displayed their lack of understanding of the key principles of mountain warfare; ordinary infantry (or armour) should fix the enemy in the valley whilst specialized light mountain infantry would try to envelop the enemy by advancing over the slopes. This was exactly what happened now; unobserved the German *Gebirgsjäger* infiltrated the steep wooded slopes on both sides of the valley and enveloped the Maquis's positions in the valley. In addition, elements of Reserve Grenadier Bataillon 179 crossed the Isère River at the railway bridge near Rognaix. It was not until around noon that the Maquisards realized the danger, but by this time the Germans had already attacked the Maquis positions in the village of Pussy where a longer battle evolved. The priest Fernand Boch commanded one of the very few mortars the Maquis had available, but was mortally wounded. Although the FFI would be able to hold Pussy until nightfall, the defence around Feissons had collapsed in the afternoon and the first blocking position was lost. As a result the AS of the Lower Tarentaise dissolved. Their boundary with the FTPF along the Isère River had turned out to be a major reason for the disaster, as the defence had been extremely ill-coordinated between both groups.

The bad news quickly reached Bulle. On the following day, 11 August, a meeting was convened at Praz-sur-Arly in Haute-Savoie between Bulle, Ortiz, the commander of the FFI forces in the Upper Tarentaise, Lungo ('Durhône'), the commander of the entire FFI force in Savoie, de Galbert and an SOE agent, Jean Rosenthal ('Cantinier'). After some debate de Galbert decided to fight a series of delaying actions at the three remaining blocking positions in the Tarentaise and hold the valley as long as possible. He ordered Bulle to dispatch his reserve, the Compagnie du Lac, to support the defence of the Tarentaise; coming from the heights this force was to harass the Germans on their left flank. Bulle and Ortiz decided to join the company. Other Resistance groups were to launch concerted diversionary attacks in the entire Savoie area.

However, de Galbert's plan crumbled all too quickly. With artillery support the Germans finally prevailed at Pussy on the morning of 11 August and during the fighting the village burst into flames. A final light resistance was offered at the second barrage around Notre-Dame-de-Briançon, but the vast majority of the FFI soon fled to the mountains north and south of Moûtiers. Bulle, Ortiz and the Compagnie du Lac had meanwhile reached the mountain village of Naves, but were unable to gain a clear picture of the situation and hence remained inactive. On 12 August the Germans prudently, but steadily, advanced through the Tarentaise and along the slopes on both sides of the valley. They held both the high and the low ground. Around noon on 13 August they reached Moûtiers and in the afternoon of the same day they took control of the road tunnel at the Etroit du Siaix. They did not lose a single man in those two days. The FFI abandoned their last two prepared blocking positions without a fight and fled into the mountains to the north of the valley.

Bulle and Ortiz were unaware of this desperate situation and thought the FFI were still preparing for a determined defence at the Etroit du Siaix. Hence on 14 August the Compagnie du Lac moved to Montgirod, a picturesque mountain village overlooking the valley from a height of about 500m. Thanks to air reconnaissance (three planes were counted that day) the Germans quickly learned about the FFI presence in Montgirod, the last Maquis concentration in the Tarentaise. As so often, the *Gebirgsjäger* displayed excellent skills manoeuvring in difficult terrain. One company approached the village from above, another frontally from Hautecour and a third (probably from Reserve Grenadier Bataillon 179) from the valley. The skirmish commenced with a heavy mortar and artillery bombardment on the village, the latter coming from the slopes on the other side of the valley. Bulle and Ortiz observed from the bell tower the fight unfolding and soon realized their Compagnie du Lac was heavily outnumbered and in danger of being encircled. However, the two officers drew different conclusions; Bulle decided to withdraw with the remaining men to the mountains at the Cormet d'Arêches before the Germans completed their encirclement of the village, whilst Ortiz and his Mission 'Union II' fought their way through, down to the valley where he intended to reorganize the dissolved FFI.

The Germans lost one man killed and one wounded at Montgirod; the FFI had two wounded whom they left in the village where the Germans later found and shot them. It would thus be an overstatement to call this fight a battle. But what followed was a tragedy. The Germans entered Montgirod with a desire for revenge; this was already the third time within the last two months they had searched this village for 'terrorists' after guerrilla activity

SKIRMISH AT MONTGIROD, 14 AUGUST 1944 (pp. 80–81)

In the second week of August 1944, the French Maquis under the charismatic ex-army officer Jean Bulle **(1)** liberated the Tarentaise Valley between Albertville and Bourg-St-Maurice in Savoie. However, only a few days later the Germans launched a major counter-offensive to retake the valley. Reserve Gebirgsjäger Bataillon 100, Reserve Grenadier Bataillon 179 and attached mountain artillery swiftly succeeded in capturing the first French defence positions and the FFI consequently dispersed to the mountains. Located 500m above the valley and already having served as an operational basis in the past weeks, the village of Montgirod was chosen as a rally point. Here Bulle hoped to stage a delaying action with his elite force, the Compagnie du Lac. This company was trained to strict military standards and consisted exclusively of officers and men from the former local *chasseurs alpins* units. The men mostly wore uniforms, but their armament was a mishmash of various, mainly British models (e.g. Sten sub-machine gun, Bren machine gun, Lee Enfield rifle). Most of the weapons came from the large Allied container drop at the Col de Saisies on 1 August 1944. The Germans detected the French forces at Montgirod relatively quickly thanks to the Luftwaffe **(2)** and possibly being betrayed by a local French shepherd. In the afternoon of 14 August 1944 the attack on the village

commenced. One *Gebirgsjäger* company advances over the heights above the village **(3)**, whilst a second one approaches from the valley. The main thrust comes from a *Gebirgsjäger* company over the plains to the west of the village **(4)**. Montgirod is shelled by mortars from the surrounding fields and artillery from the opposite side of the valley **(5)**. Bulle quickly understands that his forces are in danger of being completely encircled and consequently decides to withdraw to the mountains through the only open path to the north-east of the village **(6)**. Whilst the majority of his men reaches the safe haven at the Cormet d'Arêches, Bulle himself has to hide out on the slopes above the village for another day. The Inter-Allied Mission 'Union II' under the command of US Marine Corps Major Peter J. Ortiz chooses not to join the Maquis on their withdrawal route, but infiltrates through the German lines and descends into the valley instead **(7)**. There Ortiz hopes to reorganize the local Resistance forces and to continue the fight. He and some other members of 'Union II' surrender at Centron two days later. After the end of the fighting at Montgirod the Germans assemble the villagers on the market square and threaten to shoot the male population. In the end they back down, but burn Montgirod to the ground in reprisal.

had occurred in its vicinity. Twice the Germans had believed the villagers as they claimed ignorance, leaving the population unharmed und withdrawing without a shot being fired. In fact, the relationship between the civilians and the Resistance was not unproblematic. The Maquis had used Montgirod as an operational base and weapons cache – much to the discontent of its villagers who were scared of German reprisals. On 14 August their fears eventually became reality; after the Maquis routed, the *Gebirgsjäger* herded the villagers together and threatened to shoot the entire male population. Following a discussion between the mayor and the German commanding officer (whose identity remains unknown) the worst was to be avoided. However, it was still a nightmare; the Germans set the entire village on fire and took several hostages to Bourg-St-Maurice. They were released a few days later; the mayor and the priest of Montgirod had guaranteed with their lives that these young men would not join the Maquis.

Major Johann Kolb (1896–1977), commander of the German forces during the operation in the Tarentaise in a photo from 1942. Kolb was one of the most highly decorated officers in 157. Reserve Division and treated the US prisoners of Mission 'Union II' with great respect and gallantry. (Kolb-Radl)

Meanwhile, Bulle and his men managed to withdraw to the Cormet d'Arêches where they were able to rest. In contrast, Mission 'Union II' experienced an epic journey between 14 and 16 August. Ortiz and his men wandered around Longefoy and Centron where they were ambushed by a German column and put up a good fight for several hours against an entire company. Yet the villagers begged the US Marines to surrender; the fate of neighbouring Montgirod stood as a clear warning. Ortiz agreed and approached the German commander; the men of Mission 'Union II' expected to be shot as terrorists, but the following events turned out completely differently. The Germans refrained from any reprisals against the population of Centron, and Ortiz and the Marines were brought to the commander of the German forces in the Tarentaise, Major Kolb. Kolb received Ortiz with the greatest courtesy, praised the Marines' courageous action at Centron, and made Ortiz his guest. Both officers spent the following days together, showing each other mutual respect. After some time Kolb remarkably confessed his admiration for the Maquis's bravery and patriotism. The episode between Kolb and Ortiz showed that there was still room for humanity in this savage guerrilla war.

After the skirmish at Centron on 16 August the operations in the Tarentaise ended. The isolated German garrison descended from the Little St Bernard Pass back to Bourg-St-Maurice. The French plan to hold or at least delay the German reconquest of the Tarentaise had utterly failed, the valley was again firmly under German control. However, the high mountain ranges to the left and right remained in French hands and served as a safe refuge. On 16 August German patrols climbed the Cormet d'Arêches to penetrate the Maquis heartland. However, they were warded off and did not stage a second attempt. On 21 August the Maquis also repulsed a more serious German advance into the Chapieux Valley, together with the Cormet d'Arêches the FFI's second-largest sanctuary. These unsuccessful attacks in the side valleys showed that the long guerrilla war had also worn down and depleted German forces; they could no longer challenge the Maquis in the most remote mountain areas. During the operations for the reconquest of the Tarentaise German losses totalled about five killed, 16 wounded and seven missing. The FFI had suffered about 30 men killed in action; another 20 Resistance fighters and civilians were shot by the Germans.

AFTERMATH

On 15 August the situation changed fundamentally in southern France; 6th US Army Group with American and regular Free French forces (Seventh US Army and Armée B respectively) landed in Provence (Operation *Dragoon*) where they met only light German resistance. The situation for the Germans was critical; if the Allied forces managed to unite with their colleagues from Normandy, the 300,000 remaining German soldiers in southern France would be caught in a trap. Hitler reacted quickly and on 16 August ordered his troops to retreat from southern France. The main axis of withdrawal was the Rhône Valley; all troops to its east had to retreat to the mountain passes on the French–Italian border. However, the situation deteriorated further; the Allies had momentum on their side. With breathtaking speed armoured Task Force Butler and 36th US Infantry Division raced through the French Maritime Alps northwards along the Route Napoleon, taking the weak German garrisons in Gap and Larche prisoner with the support of the local FFI. The 36th US Infantry Division now menaced all German lines of retreat to Italy over the mountain passes. Encouraged by the Allied landing, FFI activity attained a level of intensity hitherto unseen in the area. Already

La Libération: FFI forces parade on one of the boulevards in Grenoble US troops of Task Force Butler, August 1944. (MRV)

Another photo from *La Libération* US troops of Task Force Butler in the provincial town of Die on 20 August 1944. In the French Alps the tactical cooperation between the FFI and the US forces was relatively successful, although the vast majority of German troops escaped. (MRV)

in early August German Heeresgruppe G in southern France had noted the term 'terrorist movements' was no longer valid. In reality the French Resistance would form an organized army at the rear of the army group. Indeed, on 19 August the FFI took prisoner 500 men of the German garrison in Annecy, mostly policemen from SS-Polizei Regiment 19. As a consequence 157. Reserve Division was facing complete encirclement by a combination of US forces from the south and FFI forces from the north.

The German reaction was chaotic and ill-coordinated. The 157. Reserve Division's new superior command, the Supreme Commander South-West in Italy, ordered all German units to withdraw immediately to the mountain passes on the Franco–Italian border. The execution of this order proved, however, to be much more difficult than anticipated. The divisional commander Pflaum stopped all ongoing operations against the Maquis; instead, he ordered the US forces south of Grenoble to be blocked and at the same time tried to secure the lines of withdrawal to three mountain passes: the Little St Bernard Pass, the Montgenèvre Pass, and the Mont Cenis Pass with its railway tunnel. On 21 August the last German troops withdrew from Grenoble to the east, but almost 200 men were captured by the Maquis shortly after they had left the city. Other units, such as Reserve Grenadier Bataillon 217, became FFI prisoners in the following two days during the retreat. The plan to stop the US advance south of Grenoble was also a failure. Reserve Gebirgsjäger Bataillon II/98 surrendered to FFI forces and 1st Battalion, 143rd US Infantry Regiment (36th US Infantry Division), at Vizille on 22 August. Barely a shot was fired. Most of the German officers had disgracefully abandoned the young soldiers they had been entrusted with and fought their way through to the rest of the division. On the same day FFI and American forces liberated Grenoble. Former Maquis forces from the Vercors played a considerable role here and pursued the retreating German forces in the direction of Lyon and the Franco-Italian border.

After the FFI temporarily blocked the Tarentaise again and took Briançon, the only major road open for the retreat of the bulk of the former Grenoble garrison led through the Maurienne Valley. However, this was a dangerous place to be. From the mountains FFI forces (supported by the Jedburgh Team 'Ephedrine') constantly ambushed retreating German columns in the valley. The Maquis were about to cut off the majority of 157. Reserve Division from

Generalmajor Paul Schricker (1895–1965) in the centre, the new commander of 157. Reserve Division, on one of the mountain passes following the withdrawal to the Franco-Italian border, September 1944. At the same time the 157. Reserve Division was reorganized into 157. Gebirgs Division. (Karl Hammer)

its last substantial line of retreat. It could have been an outstanding military success. However, the newly arrived 90. Panzergrenadier Division from Italy linked up with 157. Reserve Division in the Maurienne and saved the retreating German forces from a full-out disaster.

The German withdrawal saw a final peak of violence in this area. The Maurienne Valley was particularly affected where FFI forces continuously attacked retreating German columns, with individual villages changing hands several times. The Germans left a path of destruction and shot dozens of civilians in the valley. Much to the shock of many of his fellow officers Oberst Schwehr ordered the execution of Capitaine Bulle in the

Tarentaise on 23 August. Bulle had been arrested in Albertville where he had shown up in his *chasseurs alpins* uniform and tried to negotiate the peaceful surrender of the German garrison. Schwehr was in all likelihood also responsible for the execution of 28 civilian hostages at a place called Terre Noire near the Little St Bernard Pass on 28 August; the victims had been arrested during the operation in the Tarentaise in mid-August. The French also committed atrocities against German prisoners. When the murder of Bulle and a Sipo/SD mass execution of prisoners at Montluc in Lyon became public, the FFI picked out 80 prisoners (all police and Sipo/SD personnel) at Annecy and shot them on 29 August and 2 September despite attempts at intervention by the Red Cross and the general insistence of most FFI officers and the Americans that the German prisoners should be treated correctly; this was believed to be an encouragement to surrender.

The overheated situation improved only when German forces had withdrawn from French territory and a firm front line was established almost exactly along the Franco-Italian border. In the following weeks the FFI quickly transformed into the new regular Division Alpine FFI, renamed 27e Division Alpine in the autumn. It was under the command of Général Valette d'Osia, a regional Resistance fighter who had fled to Algiers in 1943 and now returned with the regular French Armée B. De Galbert and Le Ray commanded a regiment in the division, de Beauregard a battalion. With about 30,000 men the division looked strong on paper, but had to overcome serious organizational and logistical problems. As the Americans generally refused to equip FFI forces, the French had to improvise with a mishmash of uniforms and armament. Yet, the division displayed sound fighting spirit in holding the northern sector of the French Alps.

The Germans still had one clear advantage over the French in this theatre of war. They held all the mountain passes and hence the vital high ground. However, their morale was broken. The 157. Reserve Division did not perform particularly well during the retreat to the passes, losing about 2,000 men, most of them prisoners. Its reaction to the admittedly challenging twofold menace from regular US and irregular FFI forces was often disorganized. In all fairness, the division was also victim to contradictory orders from above during those dramatic days; higher command also gave the impression of being disorientated. In early September the division underwent a complete makeover and was renamed 157. Gebirgs Division. About two-thirds of the division's officer corps was replaced. Generalmajor Paul Schricker relieved Pflaum as the divisional commander, because Pflaum's performance was deemed unsatisfactory during the retreat. Oberst Schwehr was one of the few officers who kept his command. In autumn the division was reinforced by 5. Gebirgs Division and finally transferred to the Appenine front in December 1944. Owing to the harsh climatic conditions in the winter, the war in the Western Alps focused on ski patrols and only sporadic skirmishes took place. Right up to April 1945 the front remained mainly static and was merely a sideshow in the downfall of the German Reich.

In the immediate post-war years the Vercors was a contentious subject of political debate. Too many questions remained unanswered about the responsibility for the defeat in 1944 and mutual accusations between various former Resistance groups were common. Communists blamed de Gaulle for the betrayal of the Vercors and some former Maquisards criticized the performance of the military. These quarrels still have not fully ceased today, but from the 1970s onwards one particular view has finally prevailed; the

The German retreat from the French Alps, August to September 1944

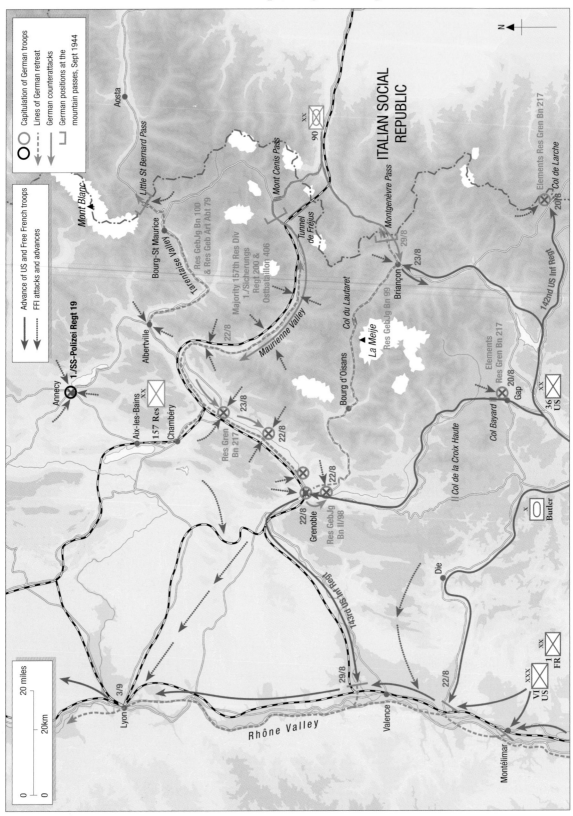

Legend:

Capitulation of German troops
Lines of German retreat
German counterattacks
German positions at the mountain passes, Sept 1944

Advance of US and Free French troops
FFI attacks and advances

1./SS-Polizei Regt 19

20 miles

20km

Key place and unit labels on map:

Aosta
Mont Blanc
Little St Bernard Pass
Bourg-St Maurice
Tarentaise Valley
Albertville
Annecy
Aix-les-Bains
Chambéry
157 Res
Res Gren Bn 217
23/8
22/8
22/8
Grenoble
Res GebJg Bn II/98
22/8
143rd US Inf Regt
Lyon
3/9
Rhône Valley
Valence
29/8
Montélimar
22/8
Die
Butler
Gap
20/8
Elements Res Gren Bn 217
Col Bayard
36 US
VI US
1 FR
Col de la Croix Haute
Bourg d'Oisans
Col du Lautaret
La Meije
Res GebJg Bn 99
Briançon
23/8
29/8
Montgenèvre Pass
Tunnel de Fréjus
Mont Cenis Pass
Maurienne Valley
Majority 157th Res Div
1./Sicherungs Regt 200 &
Ostbataillon 406
Res GebJg Bn 100
& Res Geb Art Abt 79
90
ITALIAN SOCIAL REPUBLIC
20/8 Col de Larche
Elements Res Gren Bn 217
142nd US Inf Regt

N

Vercors was a national symbol of the French Resistance in a courageous albeit tragic fight against the occupier and Vichy France. Though militarily defeated, it was morally a huge victory for the French Republic in the long term. Many Frenchmen (and foreigners) fought or even sacrificed their lives there for the values of Liberty, Equality and Fraternity.

The former French Resistance leaders in the Alps are still remembered today in the French army. Poitau ('Stéphane'), de Galbert and Bulle were all three name patrons for officers' classes at the French military academy of St Cyr. Many of them pursued a splendid military career after the war; Descour and Zeller retired as *généraux d'armée*; Huet, Le Ray and de Beauregard as *généraux de corps*. Only Geyer did not advance beyond the rank of Lieutenant-Colonel. Ironically, most of these heroes of the French Resistance had to fight irregular movements after 1945; the once hunted became the hunters. Le Ray was first deployed to Indo-China and later served twice in Algeria during the war, on his last tour as divisional commander of the 27e Division Alpine. Huet also fought as a divisional commander in Algeria. De Beauregard volunteered for Indo-China, where he had two long spells. The iconic commander of Compagnie Stéphane, Etienne Poitau, fell in a Viet Minh ambush in April 1952. Only de Galbert and Zeller fought neither in Indo-China nor in Algeria. De Galbert left the army in 1947 for personal reasons and Zeller remained in France. The one-time civil leader of the Vercors, Eugène Chavant, turned down the offer of becoming prefect for the Isère department after the liberation. He felt he had been abandoned by the Allies and de Gaulle during the desperate defence of the Vercors Republic.

In contrast to the French the military career of all their German counterparts was ruined after 1945. They returned to their civilian lives where some of them succeeded in establishing second careers, such as Kolb

François Huet as Général de Division and commander of 7e Division Mécanique Rapide in Algeria in 1958. Like so many other former leaders of the French Resistance he pursued a splendid military career after 1945. (Philippe Huet)

Young FFI fighters being instructed in the Vercors, summer 1944. Like most insurgency movements the FFI wanted to gain legal status and boost legitimacy by becoming regular forces. In France in general and in the Vercors in particular this step came too early. (IWM)

and Kneitinger who both became head teachers in schools in Bavaria. Rességuier emigrated from Germany to New York and lived there as an artist. Other former officers' fates were less happy; Schwehr committed suicide in the 1950s for unknown reasons (oddly enough the French had never opened criminal proceedings against him). Niehoff was taken prisoner by the Soviets in 1945 and perished shortly after. The daring and highly decorated Friedrich Schäfer became a modest sales representative. After 1945 all those men lived in fear of being extradited to France for war crimes. The Military Court in Lyon tried a case from 1949 to 1953 against former members of the Sipo/SD Lyon and Grenoble. Many of the defendants were sentenced to forced labour, but soon released thanks to Franco-German reconciliation. Pflaum was the only military man in the dock at this trial. Charged with complicity in murder, he was prematurely released owing to poor health; he passed away in 1972. Initially, the French authorities failed to seize two of the worst perpetrators; Knab had died in an air attack in Germany in February 1945 and Barbie had fled to Latin America. He was only caught decades later and sentenced to life imprisonment in a spectacular media-intensive trial in Lyon in 1987.

What are the general lessons on guerrilla warfare that can be drawn from the fighting in the Vercors and the other operations in the Alps in 1944? The Vercors and the Tarentaise demonstrate a common aspiration among underground movements; once they feel strong enough their aim is to hold ground and create 'liberated areas' in order to increase their standing amongst the population and also to gain legitimacy both from the occupiers and international opinion (similar to the great Chinese communist leader Mao

Tse Tung's analysis in his three stages of a 'war of national liberation'). However, in the Vercors and the Tarentaise this step was taken prematurely. Militarily the FFI could not hold the ground they had liberated. In contrast, to a great degree, the FFI in the Alps helped the Allied troops to pave the ground for the liberation of their country on a tactical level by delivering invaluable intelligence, carrying out diversionary attacks and cutting the German lines of retreat. This confirms a second rule for the deployment of irregular forces; if they are to operate in conjunction with regular forces, they must operate in support, not the other way round as in the Vercors or the Tarentaise.

On the other hand the fighting in the Vercors and the Tarentaise can be regarded as typical for the Wehrmacht in World War II: tactically and operationally brilliant (with the exception of the retreat), but inadequate on the strategic level. Fighting the insurgents was seen only as a military problem, the underlying political causes were not addressed. For example, it would have probably been wiser to recognize the FFI as combatants instead of just shooting them. This policy was intended to deter the French from joining the Maquis, but instead it deterred the FFI from surrendering. A few days or weeks later these men would re-emerge at a different place and fight the Germans again. The ruthless German behaviour in anti-partisan operations in the Alps can only partly be attributed to Nazi ideology, but was to a large degree born out of the surrounding constraints. In the spring of 1944 157. Reserve Division had protested against the burning of houses and the execution of civilians carried out by the Sipo/SD. By late summer 1944 the division's approach no longer differed fundamentally from the policy it had criticized only a few months earlier. Casualties from ambushes caused a deep hatred for the Maquis. However, more importantly, once an area was cleared of FFI fighters the Germans did not have the troops to hold the ground and the Vichy-French police forces were deemed unreliable for the job. Resorting to selective terror seemed to be the only viable option to deter the population from supplying and supporting the Maquis – with drastic consequences for both the FFI and the local population.

THE BATTLEFIELD TODAY

The Vercors is a perfect battlefield tour location. When driving along the motorway in the foothills of the mountain range the tourist signs are already there to see: 'Haut Lieu de la Résistance', the Stronghold of the Resistance. In Vassieux there are two museums: the welcoming Musée de la Résistance de Vassieux-en-Vercors in the village itself and the Mémorial de la Résistance en Vercors on the slopes above. Both are a must for anyone interested in the Vercors battle, as they give a good insight into the fighting from the French perspective. Standing on the memorial's balcony there is a spectacular view over the plains around Vassieux where the German gliders landed on 21 July 1944. Remnants of their skeletons can still be seen in Vassieux and the FFI cemetery nearby. Dozens of smaller and bigger monuments are scattered across the Vercors and remind the modern visitor of the many victims caused by the bloody events in 1944. The cemetery for the FFI near Vassieux brings an emotional touch to the entire tour. Its German counterpart is located in Dagneux to the east of Lyon where almost 20,000 German soldiers are buried, killed in the fighting in the whole of southern France in summer 1944; amongst them are also those fallen in the Vercors.

A tombstone of an *SS-Hauptscharführer* and an 18-year-old *Gebirgsjäger* at the German military cemetery at Dagneux near Lyon; both men fell on the first day of the Vercors operation. The *SS-Hauptscharführer* was in all likelihood Sipo/SD personnel. (Author's collection)

La Nécropole de la Résistance at Vassieux-en-Vercors, in remembrance of the FFI. The monument was erected by the Pionniers du Vercors, an association of former Maquisards. (Author's collection)

Apart from the museums and monuments the preservation of the battlefield is another advantage of the Vercors. Apart from the Lans and Corrençon area, very few things have changed in the past 70 years, even though the vegetation is nowadays generally denser than it was in 1944. The Vercors of 2012 closely resembles the Vercors of 1944. The mountain passes in the south-east look exactly the same as in 1944 and it is almost possible to identify the individual Maquis positions. In addition, the Vercors's natural beauty will charm and delight the visitor. It is possible to combine mountain hiking and battlefield touring in this part of the Alps. Perhaps it is worth pointing out that a visit in winter and early spring is less advisable owing to the snowy conditions.

The Resistance in the Tarentaise has attracted much less academic, popular and political interest; consequently, a museum does not exist. As in the Vercors many monuments in the villages and along the roads are reminders of the events of 1944. Today the Tarentaise has the highest density of ski resorts (such as La Plagne and Les Trois Vallées) in the world. The unattractive and noisy town of Moûtiers as well as the motorway leading through the valley make it somewhat challenging to get a sense of the past. Yet many other places such as Feissons and in particular picturesque Montgirod provide a very good insight into what the ground looked like in 1944.

BIBLIOGRAPHY

D'Arbaumont, J., *Capitaine Jean Bulle 1913–1944. Résistance en Savoie 1940–1944*, Guéniot: Langres, 1992

Béguin, A. et al., *Le Livre Noir du Vercors,* Editions Ides et Calendes: Neuchâtel, 1944

Bolle P. (ed.), *Grenoble et le Vercors. De la Résistance à la Liberation 1940–1944*, La Manufacture: Lyon, 1985

Dereymez, J.-W. (ed.), *Militaires dans la Résistance. Ain, Dauphiné, Savoie*, Anovi: Avon-les-Roches, 2010

Dreyfus, P., *Vercors. Citadelle de la Liberté*, Arthaud: Paris, new edition, 1997

Emprin, G., *Les Carnets du Capitaine Bulle. L'Homme derrière la Légende*, Fontaine de Siloé: Montmélian, 2003

Foot, M. R. D., *SOE in France. An Account of the Work of the British Special Operations Executive in France 1940–1944*, HM Stationery Office: London, 1966

Lieb, P., *Konventioneller Krieg oder NS-Weltanschauungskrieg? Kriegführung und Partisanenbekämpfung in Frankreich 1943/44*, Oldenbourg Verlag: Munich, 2007

Pearson, M., *Tears of Glory. The Betrayal of Vercors,* Macmillan: London, 1978

Thomas, G. J. & Ketley, B., *KG 200. The Luftwaffe's Most Secret Unit*, Hikoki Publications: Crowborough, 2003

Vergnon, G., *Vercors. Histoire et Mémoire d'un Maquis*, Edition de l'Atelier: Paris, 2002

——, *Résistance dans le Vercors. Histoire et Lieux de Mémoire*, Glénat: Grenoble, 2012

Note on primary sources

Primary sources on the Vercors and the Tarentaise are rather scarce. Only a handful of German military documents concerning anti-partisan operations in the French Alps have survived the war. This made the research for this book rather challenging in may ways, as the documents are scattered about in various archives, namely the Bundesarchiv-Militärarchiv in Freiburg, the WASt in Berlin and the Service Historique de la Défense in Vincennes. On the French side the documentation is much better, even though the number of written FFI documents from summer 1944 is fairly limited owing to the nature of guerrilla warfare. There are also a number of unpublished memoirs and personal reports from former Maquisards. All these documents can be found in the Archives Nationales in Paris, the departmental archives for Isère (Grenoble), Drôme (Valence) and Savoie (Chambéry) and the Service Historique de la Défense in Vincennes. The Musée de la Résistance in Vassieux and the Musée de la Résistance et de la Déportation de l'Isère in Grenoble both keep private collections. After-action reports from various Jedburgh Teams and Inter-Allied Missions as well as files regarding the planning of 'Anvil-Dragoon' and the role of the French Resistance within it can be found in the National Archives in Kew and the National Archives in Washington, DC. Unfortunately, most of the SOE files are lost. Finally, the records of French trials against German war criminals after 1945 are of particular interest. These files are stored in the Dépôt Central des Archives de la Justice Militaire in Le Blanc and are classified for 100 years or more. However, the author of this book was granted access thanks to special permission from the French Ministry of Defence.

INDEX